kiac

D1548541

Coconut
Rice
Almond
Oat
Pistachio

OCT – + 2017

ARABIAN
SEA

BAY of
BENGAL

INDIAN OCEAN

Ancient Heritage Cookies

Ancient Heritage Cookies

Gluten-Free, Whole-Grain, and Nut-Flour Treats

Luane Kohnke • Photographs by John Uher

PELICAN PUBLISHING COMPANY
GRETNA 2016

To my husband, Larry
Thank you for your steadfast help and encouragement

*The word "Pelican" and the depiction of a pelican are
trademarks of Pelican Publishing Company, Inc., and are
registered in the U.S. Patent and Trademark Office.*

Library of Congress Cataloging-in-Publication Data

Names: Kohnke, Luane, author.
Title: Ancient heritage cookies : gluten-free, whole-grain, and nut-flour
    treats / by Luane Kohnke ; photographs by John Uher.
Description: Gretna, Louisiana : Pelican Publishing Company, [2016] |
    Includes bibliographical references and index.
Identifiers: LCCN 2016017837| ISBN 9781455621316 (hardcover : alk. paper) |
    ISBN 9781455621323 (e-book)
Subjects: LCSH: Cookies. | Heirloom varieties (Plants) | Grain—Varieties. |
    Cooking (Nuts) | LCGFT: Cookbooks.
Classification: LCC TX772 .K669 2016 | DDC 641.86/54—dc23 LC record available at
https://lccn.loc.gov/2016017837

Printed in Malaysia

Published by Pelican Publishing Company, Inc.
1000 Burmaster Street, Gretna, Louisiana 70053

Contents

Acknowledgments

Many thanks to the dedicated recipe testers who baked my creations in their home kitchens and provided important feedback on all of the recipes. Although there were many testers who invested their time and energy, special thanks go to an outstanding few who contributed throughout the project: Fran Carbone, Christine Como, Beth Goehring, Sowmya Jagannath, Cindy Lindenbaum, and Rebecca Wilkins. I could not have done this without your conscientious feedback and terrific comments!

Thanks also to my colleagues at Havas Worldwide for celebrating "Cookie Mondays" with me and for eating every sample batch of cookies that I baked, providing adjectives to fuel the creative writing process, and giving feedback on taste and texture preferences. By encouraging me to bake, you created a virtuous cycle of endless treats. I am indebted to each and every one of you. You are inspirational in so many ways!

Finally, thanks to the man who never lets me down—my husband, Larry. Your active support editing and proofreading each recipe and all of the narrative sections is something that I deeply appreciate. You are the best!

Introduction

Cookies are my passion. For over thirty years, I have been baking cookies for friends, family, and work colleagues. I use these small, handheld treats to meet new people, foster deeper relationships, and simply bring everyday enjoyment to those around me. My reputation is based on this generosity of butter, flour, and sugar.

One of the things that I have observed over the years is that food is an important way to connect people across diverse cultures. Food is, after all, communal, and sharing food not only literally nurtures people but gives them a deeper cultural appreciation of each other and often opens up interesting cultural connections. Cookies invoke happy childhood memories and symbolize homemade goodness. They remind us of our family heritage and our cultural roots. It is quite remarkable that these bite-sized treats have such a strong foothold in our lives and can evoke such strong memories. Food is amazingly powerful.

Deeply rooted in ancient civilizations, and part of mankind's history for thousands of years, ancient and whole-grain flours recently have been rediscovered as healthier alternatives to all-purpose flour. In researching this phenomenon, one of the gaps I saw was that many baking recipes that claim to be whole grain use a mixture of all-purpose flour and whole-grain flour. Although these recipes are more nutritious than those using all-purpose flour alone, in my mind, they are really not whole grain.

Ancient Heritage Cookies fills this gap. It contains recipes that focus exclusively on whole-grain, ancient-grain, and nut flours. None of the recipes contain all-purpose flour. Thirteen of the fifty recipes are gluten-free—made with gluten-free grain and nut flours—and two of the recipes are vegan. The recipes have been kitchen-tested by a group of volunteers, and taste-tested by even more volunteers, to ensure that they deliver on taste, texture, and ease of preparation.

I read extensively about food and nutrition, and I am fascinated by the history of food and the way in which the domestication of crops helped establish the early civilizations that shaped today's world. Because of this, I organized the recipes in this book by the region of the world where the flour originated:

- The Fertile Crescent
- Asia and the Pacific Basin
- Mesoamerica.

I have included recipes that use the following:

- Ancient whole grains: barley, spelt, rye, kamut, amaranth
- Modern whole grains: white whole-wheat, whole-wheat pastry
- Gluten-free whole grain: oats, corn, brown rice
- Nut flours: coconut, almond, hazelnut, pistachio.

In each chapter, I have reinterpreted three classic cookies (shortbread, chocolate-chip, and brownies) with flours from that region and have included at least one variation for each. The recipes cover a broad spectrum of cookies, including molasses-rye, coconut fudge brownies, maple almond butter, apple bars, crunchy cacao nib cookies, walnut-amaranth minis, chocolate-hazelnut bars, kamut and whole-wheat shortbread, and citrus cornmeal cookies. To provide context, each chapter includes a brief history of the grains from the featured region and an overview for each of the flours that originated there.

I hope that you enjoy the recipes in this book and that at least one of them becomes a new favorite.

Happy baking!

Whole-Grain Cookie Basics

Today's consumers are focused on making healthier choices. As part of this trend, ancient grains and whole grains have been rediscovered and have become broadly included in mainstream diets.

A whole grain is a cereal grain that contains the germ, endosperm, and bran. A refined grain contains only the endosperm. Whole grains tend to have more fiber and nutrients than refined flours. The consumption of whole grains also has been linked to a decrease in risk factors for various diseases.

Ancient grains have no official definition, but they are generally considered to be grains or pseudo-grains that have been largely unchanged over the last several hundred years. They are an interesting and attractive choice to consumers because they are a bit exotic, although they are not considered healthier than modern whole grains.

Baking with whole-grain, ancient-grain, and nut flours is somewhat more nuanced than baking with all-purpose flour. The guidelines below should help you master the approach.

General Preparation Guidelines

Store Flour in the Refrigerator or Freezer

Because they contain the bran and germ of the grain, whole grains are not as shelf-stable as refined grains, i.e., they become rancid more quickly. Therefore, it is best to store these flours in airtight containers in the refrigerator or freezer. To maintain freshness, it is advised to store all nuts and nut flours in the refrigerator or freezer as well. When using these flours in baking, bring just the quantity needed to room temperature before using.

Plan to Hydrate

Because they contain the germ and bran of the grain, baked

goods made with whole-grain flours have a chewier, and sometimes a grittier, texture than refined flour. One way to mitigate this is to hydrate the flour for a few hours or overnight after the dough has been mixed. This process helps to break down or soften the bran.

For the recipes that require hydration, the amount of time required has been specified in the recipe header. This step requires a little planning in advance; but if you are anything like me, you will quickly realize that separating mixing from baking means finding two shorter timeframes rather than finding a single block of time to bake, which may actually be easier.

Resting Can Help

Finally, resting bar cookies overnight, after baking, helps the bran "disappear," giving the final baked good a less chewy texture. This is especially true for cookies made with white whole-wheat flour. This is probably the hardest tip to follow, but you will notice a difference if you do it.

Optional: Measure with a Scale

The recipes in this book show a weight as well as a volume measure for most ingredients. Using a scale is more accurate and can result in a better product. It also makes prep and cleanup faster. If you do a lot of baking or cooking, it is worth investing in a small digital scale.

For a conversion of the weights and measures I use in this book, refer to the chart on page 15.

Preparation Checklist

1. Since baking is a bit of chemistry, it is important to accurately measure all ingredients and to follow instructions carefully. Begin by reading the recipe ingredients and noting what is needed. Also read the preparation instructions, from beginning to end, once or twice. Note the equipment needed, such as baking sheets, parchment paper, mixers, rubber spatulas, cooling racks, etc. Make note of the time that may be required for chilling the dough, or if any other special preparation is required, such as toasting nuts. Many doughs

are chilled for 1 to 2 hours or overnight. Plan for this.

2. Prep all the ingredients prior to beginning the mixing process. If you anticipate what you will need and have the ingredients ready, you will find yourself moving smoothly through the entire process of creating cookies.

3. If you don't use a scale, fluff up the flour in its container. Using a spoon, scoop flour from the container and place into the measuring cup. Do not pack. Level with a straightedge. This will ensure accuracy.

4. Sift or whisk the dry ingredients as directed. This technique aerates the flour and distributes the leavening and spices evenly throughout, making the finished cookie more uniform in texture.

5. Most butter and eggs should be at room temperature (about 65° F) before beating. Room temperature butter is pliable but not soft or melted. Consult the recipe for what is required.

6. The flour mixture is usually added to the butter mixture just until all traces of flour disappear. This is called "just combined." To avoid overmixing, I turn off my mixer when there is a little bit of flour left (less than a half tablespoon), and mix it in by hand. Overmixing usually results in a tough cookie. This can be mitigated by resting the dough, but in general, go easy on mixing in the flour.

7. If instructions recommend chilling, chill for at least the minimum amount of time specified. Chilling relaxes the gluten, breaks down the bran, and helps flavors become more developed and integrated into the dough. Cookies become more tender and flavorful. Chilling also helps cookies spread less during baking. If chilled dough is too stiff to scoop or roll, let it soften for a few minutes at room temperature before placing it on the cookie sheets.

8. About 15 minutes before baking the first batch, preheat the oven to the recommended temperature. If using a convection oven, reduce the baking temperature by 25 degrees and check for doneness a bit earlier than the recipe calls for.

9. Cookies bake more evenly if they are all the same size and sufficiently spaced apart on the cookie sheets. I recommend using a cookie scoop to form equal-size dough balls. You can also use a scale to measure equal-size portions.

10. Parchment paper is recommended as a liner for cookie sheets. Cookies will not stick to parchment, making cleanup

easier. Parchment also has an insulating effect, which promotes even baking. You can also use a silicone sheet, if you prefer.

11. Cool cookies thoroughly before storing in an airtight container. Cookies that are not completely cooled before storing can become soggy and lose their shape due to trapped steam. Store each cookie variety in its own sealed container so that flavors and aromas don't mingle.

12. If you are making gluten-free cookies for someone who has celiac disease or gluten intolerance, be sure to use only gluten-free ingredients. Read the product labels carefully, and if in doubt, check with the manufacturer. If you are working in a kitchen that also has gluten ingredients in it, gluten contamination is possible. Even a few gluten-containing crumbs can be harmful to people with celiac disease or wheat allergies. To prevent gluten contamination:

• Thoroughly wash all baking equipment—including utensils, cookie sheets, and baking pans—before using them, or use an entirely different set of utensils and pans.

• Thoroughly clean all preparation surfaces, including countertops and cutting boards.

• Wipe down standing mixers and the exterior surfaces of food processors.

Freezing and Storage Tips

Freezing cookie dough or baked cookies is a great way to manage your time and serve just the quantity you need.

Freezing Dough

Most stiff cookie doughs can be frozen. Liquid batters or meringue doughs cannot be frozen.

To freeze drop cookies, scoop uniform balls of cookie dough onto cookie sheets, spacing them 1 inch apart, and freeze them until solid. Put the frozen balls into a freezer storage bag and store up to one month in the freezer.

When you are ready to bake, place frozen cookie balls on prepared cookie sheets, spacing as directed, and defrost completely before baking. You can also freeze the entire batch of dough in a sealed plastic container, defrost it in the refrigerator for several hours or overnight, and use as directed.

For slice-and-bake cookie logs, shape and wrap logs in wax paper or plastic wrap, then wrap in aluminum foil and place in a freezer storage bag. To defrost, cut the frozen dough into individual slices and defrost, or defrost the entire log in the refrigerator for several hours or overnight and use as directed.

Freezing Cookies

Be sure cookies are completely cooled before freezing.

Freeze cookies, layered between wax or parchment paper, in a freezer storage bag. If cookies are fragile, place the freezer storage bag in a baking pan or plastic container to protect the edges of the cookies.

Frozen cookies can be stored for up to one month in the freezer. To defrost, place cookies on a flat surface, in a single layer, at room temperature for about one hour.

For bar cookies, cut the pan of cookies into individual cookies, wrap each cookie in plastic wrap, and place wrapped cookies in a freezer storage bag. Alternatively, wrap the entire pan of uncut cookies in plastic wrap or aluminum foil, place it in a freezer storage bag, and freeze.

Frozen bar cookies can be stored in the freezer for 4 to 6 weeks. To defrost individual bar cookies, place unwrapped cookies on a flat surface, in a single layer, at room temperature for about one hour. For a pan of uncut cookies, defrost at room temperature for 2 to 3 hours.

Gift Packaging Ideas

Cookies can be packaged in many ways, for many occasions. Even a simple cellophane bag with a bow can transform the humblest of cookies into a special gift. Keep these general principles in mind:

- Use only food-safe packaging materials.

- Make sure the packaging is spotlessly clean before placing any cookies inside of it.
- Be sure cookies have cooled completely before packaging.
- Don't overcrowd. Cookies are fragile, and crowding may break them.
- Use parchment paper, wax paper, or paper doilies to line tins and boxes. It adds a nice touch, helps control grease stains, and also adds a little cushioning.
- Use parchment paper to separate cookie layers, or use cupcake papers to hold and separate different cookie varieties. The paper will keep flavors separate and prevent cookies from sticking together. It also adds cushioning.

Tins

Tins are my personal favorite for packaging, mailing, or transporting cookies. They are sturdy enough for mailing and are usually airtight. You can buy food-safe tins in a variety of shapes and sizes at local cake and decorating shops, online, or even at grocery stores during the holiday season. Before using, wash tins thoroughly and air-dry.

Boxes

Boxes are another great gift packaging idea. They come in a variety of colors, shapes, and sizes. Some have transparent tops to display the treats inside. You can also find clear, food-safe, acetate boxes and cylinders. Choose a box that will fit the cookies neatly and snugly. After filling, secure the box with ribbon or tape. Food-safe boxes can be found at local craft stores or craft departments, as well as online.

Bags

Cellophane bags are a great option to package a stack of cookies for a special gift or a party favor. Bags come in a variety of colors and prints. Most are from Wilton Industries and can be found in craft stores or department stores, at grocery stores, or online. After filling the bag, secure the top with a colorful ribbon or tie.

Weights and Measures—Volume Equivalents (In Grams)

Sugars:

Ingredient	1 Cup =	1/4 Cup =
Granulated Sugar	200	50
Dark Brown Sugar, Packed	220	55
Light Brown Sugar, Packed	220	55
Powdered Sugar	125	31

Flours:

Ingredient	1 Cup =	1/4 Cup =
Almond Flour	112	28
Whole-Wheat Flour	130	33
Pastry Flour	130	33
Spelt	120	30
Kamut	120	30
Rye	120	30
Brown-Rice Flour	160	40
Rolled Oats	90	23
Oat Flour	120	30
Steel-Cut Oats	156	39
Coconut Flour	112	28
Corn Flour	116	29
Cornmeal	150	38
Amaranth	120	30
Amaranth Seeds	208	52
Barley Flour	120	30

Cocoa:

Ingredient	1 Cup =	1/4 Cup =
Dutch-Processed	88	22
Regular	82	21
Nibs	136	34

Nuts:

Ingredient	1 Cup =	1/4 Cup =
Pecans, Chopped	109	27
Walnuts, Chopped	118	30
Peanuts	155	39
Pistachios	125	31
Whole Almonds	140	35
Sliced Almonds	112	28
Hazelnuts	115	29

Dried Fruits:

Ingredient	1 Cup =	1/4 Cup =
Cranberries	160	40
Cherries	160	40
Blueberries	184	46
Apricots	177	44
Unsweetened Coconut	80	20
Sweetened Coconut	120	30
Zante Currants	160	40

Chocolate Chips:

Ingredient	1 Cup =	1/4 Cup =
Semi, 60%, mini	163	41
White (scant cup)	156	39

Other:

Ingredient	1 Cup =	1/4 Cup =
Lemon Curd	304	76
Mascarpone	224	56
Honey	272	68
Peanut Butter	256	64
Almond Butter	272	68
Cashew Butter	240	60
Maple Syrup	316	79
Cornstarch	128	32

BLACK SEA

MEDITERRANEAN
SEA

RED SEA

PERSIAN
GULF

Spelt
Barley
Wheat
Kamut
Rye
Hazelnut

The Fertile Crescent

The Fertile Crescent is often called the cradle of civilization because of its importance to the origins of agriculture and the spread of humanity. It includes the area between and around the Euphrates and Tigris Rivers, which is considered to be the ancient civilization of Mesopotamia. It is bordered by mountain ranges to the north and deserts to the south, with the Caspian and Black Seas to the north, the Mediterranean and Red Seas to the west, and the Indian Ocean and Persian Gulf to the south and east. Today, countries with significant territory within this region include Iraq, Kuwait, Syria, Lebanon, Jordan, Israel, Cyprus, and Egypt, as well as southeastern Turkey and western Iran.

This region's diverse climates and dramatic range of elevation gave rise to many species of edible plants. In ancient times, it had a greater amount of biodiversity than either Europe or northern Africa. It was home to several Neolithic-era crops dating back to about 10,000 BC, including einkorn—the progenitor of every variety of wheat grown today. It was also home to emmer, spelt, barley, rye, and kamut.

The recipes in this chapter use whole-grain flours that have their roots in this ancient civilization: white whole-wheat flour, whole-wheat pastry flour, spelt, barley, rye, and kamut. The chapter also includes recipes with hazelnut flour, which originated just north and west of this region in Turkey, Azerbaijan, Italy, Greece, and Georgia.

White Whole-Wheat Flour

White whole-wheat flour is a variety of whole-wheat flour that is ground from hard, white whole-wheat. White whole-wheat has a lighter color and milder taste than traditional whole-wheat flour. It has the same nutritional benefits, as well as the same nutty flavor and distinctive chew, as traditional whole-wheat.

Top row: rye flour, spelt; middle row: hazelnut flour, barley flour, kamut; bottom row: whole-wheat pastry flour, white whole-wheat flour

White whole-wheat varieties, currently grown in the USA, were developed in the 1970s and 1980s by crossbreeding strains of red wheat. Today, white whole-wheat accounts for 10-15 percent of the total United States wheat crop. Used in a wide range of baking, it is grown from Texas, north through Kansas, and into Nebraska.

For recipes calling for white whole-wheat flour, use a fine-grind to medium-grind flour. The grind may have some flakes of bran or specs of germ, but generally it should be a smooth, tan-colored version of whole-wheat flour. In testing my recipes, I used both King Arthur 100% White Whole-Wheat Flour and Hodgson Mills White Whole-Wheat Flour, which are medium-grind flours.

Whole-Wheat Pastry Flour

Whole-wheat pastry flour is made from soft wheat, which is a plumper wheat berry than hard wheat. Soft wheat is also a winter-wheat variety, meaning that it is planted in the fall and "winters over" in the field in a state of dormancy. It is harvested in the late spring or early summer. In the USA, soft wheat is grown where the winter is less severe, primarily east of the Mississippi River and in the northern Pacific states.

Graham flour is the same wheat as whole-wheat pastry flour. It is just cold-stone ground. Today, mills that sell graham flour are usually selling whole-wheat pastry flour.

Whole-wheat pastry flour has more carbohydrates and less protein than white whole-wheat flour—and, thus, less gluten-forming ability. It imparts a distinct tenderness, rather than chew, to cookies. I use whole-wheat pastry flour in many recipes to impart a finer texture and more tender crumb than white whole-wheat flour or spelt.

Spelt

Spelt is a considered a cousin or sibling to einkorn and emmer, the ancient progenitors of today's wheat. In fact, spelt is often referred to as one of the three original ancient grain varieties and dates back to about 6000 BC. It is higher in fiber and protein than wheat and has a sweeter, nuttier flavor. It has a smooth texture and is a pleasure to bake with. It is very easy to find in the health-food or organic section of most grocery stores.

Spelt is extremely water-soluble, and although it contains more protein (gluten) than wheat, baked goods made with spelt have a more fragile structure because the gluten is more delicate. Spelt readily absorbs liquid but also releases it when mixed. Overnight refrigeration of dough helps to stabilize and absorb the liquid, making cookies less likely to spread excessively when baked.

Spelt has become my new go-to whole-grain flour. You will find it used throughout this book, on its own or in combination with other flours.

Barley Flour

Barley is one of the world's oldest cultivated crops, dating back to 10,000 BC, which is about the same time that wheat began to be cultivated. Barley is a very hardy grain, grown in multiple climates, from the deserts of Africa to the Arctic, in areas that are too dry or too cold for wheat.

Barley was brought to the Americas by Christopher Columbus and began to be cultivated in the Americas in the 1600s. Today it is grown in twenty-seven states. Much of the United States' crop is used for malt, a key ingredient in beer and whiskey.

It has a mild, nutty taste, and unlike other whole-grain flours, it has no gritty texture. Although it is high in protein, the gluten that it produces is unsuitable for building structure in baked goods, so it is usually paired with whole-wheat flour in a fifty-fifty ratio.

Rye Flour

Rye is commonly believed to have originated about five thousand years ago in nearby Asia Minor. However, there is some evidence that it may have originated earlier in the Euphrates Valley of the Fertile Crescent. A very hardy grain that can survive extreme cold and dry conditions, it arrived in North America with the early settlers in the 1600s.

Rye is high in fiber and rich in nutrients but has less gluten than wheat. It has a sweet, grassy flavor and is high in enzymes that convert starch to sugars, resulting in a faintly tacky texture in baked goods.

Rye is milled and then sifted to produce flour with different levels of germ and bran, including light, medium, dark, and pumpernickel rye. The recipes in this book call for dark rye, but light or medium rye can be substituted.

Kamut

Kamut, also called Khorasan or Oriental wheat, is a relative of durum or emmer wheat, which is the hardest of all wheats. Kamut was originally thought to date back to ancient Egypt, but its origin there is now believed to have been more recent. It has a sweet, buttery flavor, strong gluten content, and its grain is twice the size of modern wheat.

Kamut is a registered trademark variety of Khorasan wheat. It was registered with the US Patent and Trademark Office in 1990 by Mack and Bob Quinn to preserve its integrity. It can be found in specialty flour sections and online at Bob's Red Mill and Nuts.com. Kamut can be substituted one-for-one for wheat flour.

Hazelnut Flour

Hazelnuts, or filberts, have been found in Mesolithic sites in Europe dating back to 7000 BC. The Romans cultivated hazelnuts, and are thought to have cultivated them in Britain. They are rich in protein and unsaturated fats and have a balanced mixture of vitamins and minerals. Hazelnuts pair well with chocolate and are used in confections, cakes, tortes, and in a variety of products such as Frangelico liqueur and Nutella spread.

Hazelnut flour imparts a deep aromatic nuttiness and intense richness to baked goods. It is naturally gluten-free. In the USA, most hazelnuts are grown in Oregon and harvested in late September and early October.

Hazelnut flour is readily available from King Arthur Flour, Bob's Red Mill, and Nuts.com. It should be stored in an airtight container in the freezer. It is also easy to make by grinding hazelnuts in a nut chopper or food processer.

Whole Wheat

Rye

Molasses-Spice Cookies

Chilling time: 3 hours or overnight
Makes about 40 cookies

This bold molasses-rye cookie is an irresistible crowd pleaser. To quote a taste tester, "the chewy texture is perfect, the flavor brings back fond memories, and you can't eat just one." The aroma of these cookies will transport you to the winter holidays.

In a medium bowl, sift together flours, baking soda, salt, and spices. Set aside.

In the large bowl of an electric mixer, with speed set to high, beat butter and sugars 1 to 2 minutes, until light and fluffy. Add egg and molasses. Beat 1 to 2 minutes, until light and fluffy. Reduce mixer speed to low, and add flour mixture. Mix until smooth. Cover and chill for 3 hours or overnight.

Preheat oven to 350°F/180°C/ Gas Mark 4. Line cookie sheets with parchment paper.

Using a medium cookie scoop, such as #60, form 2 teaspoons of dough into 1-inch balls. Roll tops in extra granulated sugar. Place on prepared sheets, spacing about 2 inches apart. Bake 12 to 14 minutes, until tops are cracked and cookies are firm to touch. Cool for 2 minutes on cookie sheets. Transfer cookies, still on parchment, to wire racks to cool completely.

Store cookies in an airtight container, at room temperature, for up to 1 week.

INGREDIENTS

1 cup white whole-wheat flour (130 grams)
⅔ cup whole-grain dark rye flour (80 grams)
½ teaspoon baking soda
½ teaspoon salt
1½ teaspoons ground ginger
1 teaspoon ground cinnamon
½ teaspoon ground allspice
8 tablespoons (1 stick) unsalted butter, room temperature (113 grams)
½ cup packed dark brown sugar (110 grams)
¼ cup granulated sugar (50 grams)
1 large egg, room temperature
2 tablespoons molasses
Extra granulated sugar, for rolling

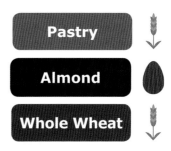

Miniature Jam Sandwich Cookies

Chilling time: 2 hours or overnight
Makes about 60 unfilled cookies or 30 filled sandwich cookies

Apricot or strawberry jam is a great pairing for these English afternoon-tea-party-inspired cookies. They are charming and petite, with an excellent texture due to their triple flour combination. Their buttery flavor also makes them great served without any filling.

In a medium bowl, whisk together flours and salt. Set aside.

In the large bowl of an electric mixer, with speed set to high, beat butter and sugar about 2 minutes, until light and fluffy. Beat in extracts until just combined. Reduce mixer speed to low, and gradually add flour mixture. Mix until just incorporated. Dough will be crumbly. Knead with hands and gather together to form a disk. Wrap in wax paper or plastic wrap. Chill at least 2 hours or overnight, for flours to hydrate.

Preheat oven to 350°F/180°C/Gas Mark 4. Line cookie sheets with parchment paper.

Roll dough between sheets of wax paper to ¼-inch thickness and cut with 1-inch, round cookie cutter. Place cookies on prepared sheets, spacing 1 inch apart. Bake for 8 to 10 minutes, until light golden brown. Cool for 1 minute on cookie sheets. Transfer cookies, still on parchment, to wire racks to cool completely.

Just before serving, spread ½ teaspoon of preserves over flat side of half of the cookies. Sandwich with another cookie. Serve filled cookies immediately.

Store unfilled cookies in an airtight container, at room temperature, for up to one week.

INGREDIENTS

¾ cup whole-wheat pastry flour (98 grams)
¾ cup almond flour (84 grams)
½ cup white whole-wheat flour (65 grams)
½ teaspoon fine sea salt
8 tablespoons (1 stick) unsalted butter, room temperature (113 grams)
⅓ cup packed light brown sugar (73 grams)
1 teaspoon pure vanilla extract
½ teaspoon pure almond extract
½ cup apricot or strawberry preserves, stirred (144 grams)

Baker's Note: If dough is too stiff to roll, let it sit for a few minutes, at room temperature, until it becomes more pliable.

Rosemary-Orange Chocolate-Chip Cookies

Chilling time: 2 hours or overnight
Makes about 30 cookies

These crisp and delicate chocolate-chip cookies are delightfully complex and sophisticated. The rosemary and orange give these savory, crisp cookies an adult twist. The slightly nutty flavor of the barley flour shines through the bittersweet chocolate, making these a wonderful chocolate-chip cookie option.

In a medium bowl, sift together flours, baking powder, baking soda, and salt. Set aside.

In the large bowl of an electric mixer, with speed set to high, beat butter and sugars, 1 to 2 minutes, until light and fluffy. Add egg and vanilla extract. Beat 1 to 2 minutes, until light and fluffy. Add rosemary and orange zest. Mix until evenly distributed. Set mixer speed to low. Add flour mixture gradually and mix until just combined. Add chocolate chips. Mix until just combined. Cover and chill for 2 hours or overnight.

Preheat oven to 350°F/180°C/Gas Mark 4. Line cookie sheets with parchment paper.

Using a medium scoop, such as #50, form 1 tablespoon of dough into 1¼-inch balls. Place on prepared sheets, spacing about 2 inches apart. Bake for 10 to 14 minutes, until deep golden brown. Cool for 1 minute on cookie sheets. Transfer cookies, still on parchment, to wire racks to cool completely.

Store cookies in an airtight container, at room temperature, for up to 1 week.

INGREDIENTS

½ cup plus 2 tablespoons white whole-wheat flour (81 grams)
½ cup whole-grain barley flour (60 grams)
½ teaspoon baking powder
¼ teaspoon baking soda
⅛ teaspoon fine sea salt
8 tablespoons (1 stick) unsalted butter, room temperature (113 grams)
½ cup granulated sugar (100 grams)
¼ cup packed light brown sugar (55 grams)
1 large egg, room temperature
1 teaspoon pure vanilla extract
1 tablespoon finely chopped fresh rosemary
1 teaspoon finely chopped or grated orange zest
1½ cups bittersweet (60% cacao) chocolate chips (245 grams)

Double-Chocolate Fruit and Nut Brownies

Makes 16 brownies

The cherry-almond combination in these chocolate brownies is perfect, adding little bursts of flavor in every bite. The only way these exquisitely moist, chocolaty, fruit- and nut-filled brownies could be better is served with your favorite ice cream.

Preheat oven to 350°F/180°C/Gas Mark 4. Line an 8x8-inch baking pan with aluminum foil, leaving a 2-inch overhang on two opposite edges. Cut a piece of parchment to fit the bottom. Lightly oil the parchment and the sides of the pan.

In a medium bowl, sift together flour and baking powder. Set aside.

In the top of a double-boiler, over simmering water, melt unsweetened chocolate and butter. Stir constantly until chocolate and butter are fully combined and mixture is smooth. Remove from heat and cool to room temperature.

In the large bowl of an electric mixer, with speed set to high, combine eggs, sugar, salt, vanilla, and almond extract. Beat 2 to 3 minutes, until mixture thickens and becomes pale in color. Using a rubber spatula, fold chocolate mixture into the egg mixture. Be careful to not deflate the batter. With the rubber spatula, fold in flour mixture in two portions. Then carefully fold in cherries, almonds, and chocolate chips, stirring until smooth. Spoon evenly into prepared pan.

Bake for 25 to 35 minutes, until the top is firm to touch. Remove from oven, place on a wire rack, and cool completely in the pan. When ready to serve, using the foil overhang, lift uncut brownies from pan. Cut into 16 servings.

Store brownies in an airtight container, at room temperature, for up to 3 days.

INGREDIENTS

¾ cup white whole-wheat flour (102 grams)
½ teaspoon baking powder
3 ounces unsweetened chocolate (85 grams)
8 tablespoons (1 stick) unsalted butter (113 grams)
4 large eggs, room temperature
1¼ cups granulated sugar (250 grams)
½ teaspoon salt
1 teaspoon pure vanilla extract
½ teaspoon pure almond extract
⅓ cup dried cherries, coarsely chopped (59 grams)
⅓ cup toasted whole almonds, chopped (53 grams)
¾ cup bittersweet (60% cacao) chocolate chips (122 grams)

Baker's Note: For a hyper-cherry flavor, substitute 1 teaspoon of cherry flavoring for the almond extract.

Chocolate-Vanilla Malt Cookies

Spelt

Barley

Chilling time: 2 hours or overnight
Makes about 24 cookies

These deceptively plain-looking cookies hide a sweet, fudgy, chocolate-vanilla malt flavor that you will love at first bite. They are crispy, but with a slightly chewy texture that comes from the malted milk powder. You can use unsweetened regular cocoa or a blend of unsweetened regular and Dutch cocoa such as King Arthur Flour's triple cocoa blend. Enjoy these cookies served as an accompaniment to milk or vanilla ice cream.

In a medium bowl, sift together flours, baking powder, baking soda, and salt. Set aside.

In the large bowl of an electric mixer, with speed set to high, beat butter and sugar 1 to 2 minutes, until light and fluffy. Add cocoa and malt powders. Beat until incorporated. Add egg and vanilla extract. Beat 1 to 2 minutes, until light and fluffy. Set mixer speed to low. Add flour mixture gradually and mix until just combined. Add chocolate chips. Mix until just combined. Cover and chill for 2 hours or overnight.

Preheat oven to 350°F/180°C/ Gas Mark 4. Line cookie sheets with parchment paper.

Using a medium scoop, such as #50, form 1 tablespoon of dough into 1¼-inch balls. Place on prepared sheets, spacing about 2 inches apart. Bake for 10 to 12 minutes, until just firm to touch. Cool for 1 minute on cookie sheets. Transfer cookies, still on parchment, to wire racks to cool completely.

Store cookies in an airtight container, at room temperature, for up to 1 week.

INGREDIENTS

⅔ cup spelt flour (80 grams)
⅓ cup whole-grain barley flour (40 grams)
½ teaspoon baking powder
¼ teaspoon baking soda
⅛ teaspoon salt
8 tablespoons (1 stick) unsalted butter, room temperature (113 grams)
½ cup granulated sugar (100 grams)
¼ cup unsweetened cocoa powder (20 grams)
3 tablespoons plain malted milk powder (21 grams)
1 large egg, room temperature
1½ teaspoons pure vanilla extract
1 cup milk chocolate chips (163 grams)

Baker's Note: Malted milk powder contains milk. Malt powder does not. You can use either, but the texture and chew will differ.

Kamut and Whole-Wheat Shortbread Cookies

Chilling time: 2 hours or overnight
Makes about 40 cookies

Kamut, also called Khorasan wheat, is an ancient grain that is believed to have its origins in Egypt. Kamut flour has a naturally buttery flavor, and whole-wheat flour has a slightly nutty flavor, making them the perfect pair for a shortbread cookie. With only five ingredients, this one-bowl recipe is quick and easy to prepare.

In a medium bowl, sift together flours and salt. Whisk in sugar. Drop butter onto flour mixture. Using a pastry cutter, cut in butter until crumbly and mixture resembles flakes. Knead with hands until pliable. Gather together, cover, and chill for 2 hours or overnight.

Preheat oven to 350°F/180°C/Gas Mark 4. Line cookie sheets with parchment paper.

Using a small cookie scoop, such as #100, form 1¾ teaspoons of dough into ¾-inch balls. Place onto prepared sheets, spacing about 1 inch apart. Gently flatten to about ⅓-inch thickness. Sprinkle tops with raw sugar, if desired. Bake for 10 to 12 minutes, until edges are golden brown. Transfer cookies, still on parchment, to wire racks to cool completely.

Store cookies in an airtight container, at room temperature, for up to 3 days.

INGREDIENTS

¾ cup plus 2 tablespoons kamut flour (105 grams)
¾ cup white whole-wheat flour (102 grams)
¾ teaspoon fine kosher salt
¾ cup plus 2 tablespoons powdered sugar (108 grams)
12 tablespoons (1 ½ sticks) unsalted butter, cold, cut into ¼-inch cubes (170 grams)
Raw sugar, such as turbindo, for sprinkling (optional)

Fig and Walnut Cookies

Chilling time: 2 hours or overnight
Makes about 40 cookies

Fragrant spices combine with figs and walnuts to make this light and chewy cookie a delightful treat. I use dried Black Mission figs, but dried Calimyrna figs, which are somewhat sweeter, can be substituted.

In a medium bowl, sift together flour, baking soda, baking powder, salt, and spices. Set aside.

In the large bowl of an electric mixer, with speed set to high, beat butter and maple syrup for 1 to 2 minutes, until light and fluffy. Add egg and vanilla. Beat about 2 minutes, until combined. Mixture will look curdled as you start to mix, but that's all right. Reduce mixer speed to low. Gradually add flour mixture and mix until just incorporated. Add figs and walnuts. Mix until just combined. Cover and chill for 2 hours or overnight, for flours to hydrate.

Preheat oven to 350°F/180°C/ Gas Mark 4. Line cookie sheets with parchment paper.

Using a medium cookie scoop, such as #60, form 2 teaspoons of dough into 1-inch balls. Place on prepared sheets, spacing about 2 inches apart. Flatten to ⅓-inch thickness. Bake for 10 to 14 minutes, until golden brown and firm to touch. Transfer cookies, still on parchment, to wire racks to cool completely.

Store cookies in an airtight container, at room temperature, for up to 3 days.

INGREDIENTS

1 cup plus 2 tablespoons whole-wheat pastry flour (144 grams)
½ teaspoon baking soda
¼ teaspoon baking powder
¼ teaspoon salt
½ teaspoon ground cardamom
¼ teaspoon ground cinnamon
⅛ teaspoon ground nutmeg
8 tablespoons (1 stick) unsalted butter, room temperature (113 grams)
¼ cup maple syrup, Grade A medium amber or dark amber (79 grams)
1 large egg, room temperature
1 teaspoon pure vanilla extract
1 cup loosely packed, coarsely chopped dried Black Mission figs (184 grams)
1 scant cup toasted walnuts, coarsely chopped (114 grams)

Baker's Note: Do not substitute fresh figs, as they contain more water than dried figs and will add too much moisture to the dough.

Gooey Pecan-Pie Bars

Makes 16 bars

I was once asked by a colleague if I could make a "nutty pecan-pie bar with a bourbon-maple flavor." That request inspired this recipe. It uses whole-wheat pastry flour for a tender, crumbly crust.

Preheat oven to 350°F/180°C/ Gas Mark 4. Line the bottom and sides of an 8x8-inch baking pan with aluminum foil, leaving a 2-inch overhang on two opposite edges. Lightly oil the bottom and the sides of the pan.

In a medium bowl, sift together the flour, cornstarch, baking powder, and salt. Set aside.

In the large bowl of an electric mixer, with speed set to high, beat butter and cream cheese 1 to 2 minutes, until smooth. Add powdered sugar. Beat until combined. Set mixer speed to low. Gradually add flour mixture until just combined. Mixture will be a gooey paste.

Drop mixture into prepared pan. Using a knife, spread mixture into an even layer. Pierce with a fork. Bake for 12 to 16 minutes, until crust is set and light golden brown. Edges should

be a shade darker. Remove from oven. Set pan on rack to cool while filling is prepared.

Clean mixer bowl and blades. In a medium bowl, combine chopped pecans and flour. Toss to lightly coat. Set aside.

In the large bowl of the electric mixer, with speed set to high, beat the butter and brown sugar, about 1 minute, until smooth. Add eggs, one at a time. Beat 2 to 3 minutes, until light and fluffy. Add the salt, corn syrup, bourbon, and extracts. Beat about 1 minute, until smooth. Set mixer speed to low. Add heavy cream, and mix until combined. Add pecan-flour mixture. Mix until evenly distributed. Pour pecan mixture evenly over crust.

Bake for 30 to 40 minutes, until filling is firm and dark golden brown. Remove from oven, place on wire rack, and cool completely in the pan. When ready to serve, using the foil overhang, lift uncut bars from pan. Cut into 16 servings.

Store bars in an airtight container, at room temperature or in the refrigerator, for up to 5 days.

INGREDIENTS

Crust
½ cup whole-wheat pastry flour (65 grams)
2 tablespoons cornstarch (16 grams)
⅛ teaspoon baking powder
⅛ teaspoon salt
4 tablespoons (½ stick) unsalted butter, room temperature (78 grams)
2 ounces cream cheese, room temperature (57 grams)
⅓ cup powdered sugar (42 grams)

Filling
1⅓ cups whole pecans, coarsely chopped (145 grams)
1 tablespoon whole-wheat pastry flour (8 grams)
4 tablespoons (½ stick) unsalted butter, room temperature (57 grams)
½ cup packed dark brown sugar (110 grams)
3 large eggs, room temperature
⅛ teaspoon salt
⅔ cup dark corn syrup
1½ tablespoons regular or honey-flavored bourbon
¾ teaspoon pure vanilla extract
⅛ teaspoon pure maple extract
2½ tablespoons heavy cream

Baker's Note: Do not line pan bottom with parchment paper, as the filling will seep underneath it.

Double-Chocolate Peppermint Cookies

Chilling time: 2 hours or overnight
Makes about 40 cookies

This special recipe is good any time of the year for the chocolate-peppermint craver in your life. This crispy, chewy cookie is packed with extra chocolate and delivers a solid peppermint flavor. I use King Arthur Flour's double-Dutch dark cocoa to get a dark, rich color and deep chocolaty taste.

In a medium bowl, sift together flour, cocoa, baking powder, baking soda, and salt. Set aside.

In the large bowl of an electric mixer, with speed set to high, beat butter and brown sugar 1 to 2 minutes, until light and fluffy. Add egg, vanilla, and peppermint extract. Beat about 1 minute, until combined. Set mixer speed to low. Add the flour mixture and mix until just combined. Add chocolate chips. Mix until combined. Cover and chill for 2 hours or overnight, for flour to hydrate.

Preheat oven to 350°F/180°C/Gas Mark 4. Line cookie sheets with parchment paper.

Using a medium cookie scoop, such as #60, form 2 teaspoons of dough into 1¼-inch balls. Place on prepared sheets, spacing about 2 inches apart. Bake for 10 to 12 minutes, until cookies are firm to touch. Cool for 2 minutes on cookie sheets. Transfer cookies, still on parchment, to wire racks to cool completely.

Store cookies in an airtight container, at room temperature, for up to 3 days.

INGREDIENTS

1 cup spelt flour (120 grams)
¼ cup Dutch-processed cocoa powder (double-Dutch dark cocoa preferred) (22 grams)
½ teaspoon baking powder
¼ teaspoon baking soda
¼ teaspoon fine sea salt
8 tablespoons (1 stick) unsalted butter, room temperature (113 grams)
¾ cup packed light brown sugar (165 grams)
1 large egg, room temperature
¾ teaspoon pure vanilla extract
¾ teaspoon pure peppermint extract
1¼ cups coarsely chopped bittersweet (60% cacao) or semisweet chocolate chips or bars (204 grams)

Maple Almond-Butter Cookies

Makes about 48 cookies

Made with whole-wheat pastry flour, these yummy vegan cookies have a hint of graham cracker sweetness. The almond butter and maple syrup give these chewy cookies a sweet, nutty flavor, boosted by the vanilla and almond extract.

Preheat the oven to 350°F/180°C/Gas Mark 4. Line cookie sheets with parchment paper.

In a medium bowl, sift together pastry flour, baking soda, and salt. Set aside.

In a large bowl, using a large spoon, combine almond butter, maple syrup, oil, and extracts. Mix until well blended. In 3 batches, add flour mixture to almond butter mixture. Stir until just combined. Stir in chopped almonds. Let sit about 5 minutes.

Using a small cookie scoop, such as #100, form 1¾ teaspoons of dough into ¾-inch balls and place on prepared sheets, spacing about 2 inches apart. Flatten each ball to about ⅓-inch thickness. Bake for 10 to 12 minutes, until golden brown. Cool for 2 minutes on cookie sheets. Transfer cookies, still on parchment, to wire racks to cool completely.

Store cookies in an airtight container, at room temperature, for up to one week.

Pastry

INGREDIENTS

1 cup plus 2 tablespoons whole-wheat pastry flour (144 grams)
½ teaspoon baking soda
½ teaspoon salt
½ cup natural almond butter (136 grams)
½ cup maple syrup, Grade A medium amber or dark amber (158 grams)
3 tablespoons extra-light or extra-virgin olive oil
½ teaspoon pure vanilla extract
½ teaspoon pure almond extract
½ cup whole almonds, chopped (82 grams)

Baker's Note: For a lighter almond flavor, reduce the almond extract to ¼ teaspoon. Olive oil cookies bake differently than butter-based cookies. They will appear very moist at first and become firm to touch while baking. This dough does not freeze well, but once baked, the cookies can be frozen.

Lemon Drops

Chilling time: overnight
Makes about 24 cookies

If you like lemonade, you will love these deliciously light and delicate lemon drops. Lemon oil plus lemon peel and lemon juice give these cookies their lemon punch. I use Boyajian lemon oil, which can be found in gourmet stores or online. For a variation, I sometimes substitute lime or orange oil, peel, and juice.

In medium bowl, sift together flour and cornstarch. Set aside.

In the large bowl of an electric mixer, with speed set to high, beat butter and powdered sugar 1 to 2 minutes, until light and fluffy. Mix in lemon juice, lemon zest, and lemon oil, until combined. Set mixer speed to low. Gradually add flour mixture. Mix until smooth. Cover and chill overnight.

Preheat oven to 350°F/180°C/ Gas Mark 4. Line cookie sheets with parchment paper.

Using a small cookie scoop, such as #100, form 1¾ teaspoons of dough into ¾-inch balls. Place on prepared sheets, spacing about 1 inch apart. Bake for 12 to 15 minutes, until pale golden brown on top and lightly browned on bottom. Cool for 2 minutes on cookie sheets. Transfer cookies, still on parchment, to wire racks. Cool for 5 more minutes. Dust with powdered sugar. Cool completely. If desired, just before serving, dust again with powdered sugar, or coat completely by rolling in powdered sugar.

Store cookies in an airtight container, at room temperature, for up to 5 days.

INGREDIENTS

¾ cup plus 2 tablespoons spelt flour (105 grams)
¼ cup cornstarch (32 grams)
8 tablespoons (1 stick) unsalted butter, room temperature (113 grams)
¼ cup powdered sugar (32 grams)
1 tablespoon fresh lemon juice
½ teaspoon packed, finely chopped or grated lemon zest
¼ teaspoon lemon oil (or substitute ½ teaspoon pure lemon extract plus additional ½ teaspoon packed, finely chopped or grated lemon zest)
Extra powdered sugar, sifted, for dusting and rolling

Spelt

Dark Chocolate Wafers with Ginger Cream

Chilling time: 1 hour or overnight
Makes about 24 unfilled cookies or 12 filled sandwich cookies

One of my favorite combinations is dark chocolate with a gingery kick, so these sandwich cookies are exactly the right combo for me. I use King Arthur Flour's double-Dutch dark cocoa, which is a combination of regular Dutch-process cocoa and black cocoa, for an extra dark color. If you want a simple, sweet chocolate treat, eat them plain, or sprinkle with vanilla sugar. (See Baker's Note below for vanilla sugar preparation.)

In a medium bowl, sift together flour, cocoa, baking soda, and salt. Set aside.

In the large bowl of an electric mixer, with speed set to high, beat butter and sugars, 1 to 2 minutes, until light and fluffy. Add vanilla and egg yolk. Beat 1 to 2 minutes, until light and fluffy. Reduce mixer speed to low. Add flour mixture and mix until smooth. Shape into a disk, wrap in wax paper or plastic wrap, and chill for at least 1 hour or overnight.

Preheat oven to 350°F/180°C/ Gas Mark 4. Line cookie sheets with parchment paper.

Roll dough between sheets of wax paper to ¼-inch thickness. Cut with 1½-inch round cookie cutter. Place cookies on prepared cookie sheets, spacing about 2 inches apart. Bake for 8 to 10 minutes, until cookies puff and tops begin to crack. Cool for 2 minutes on cookie sheets. Transfer cookies, still on parchment, to wire racks to cool completely. Serve plain, sprinkled with vanilla sugar, or fill with ginger cream before serving.

For filling: Just before serving, in a small bowl, combine the mascarpone cheese and powdered sugar. Mix by hand, with a spoon, until smooth. Add the ginger. Mix until combined. Spread ½ teaspoon over flat side of half of the cookies. Sandwich with another cookie. Serve filled cookies immediately.

Store unfilled cookies in an airtight container, at room temperature, for up to 5 days.

INGREDIENTS

¾ cup spelt flour (90 grams)
¼ cup unsweetened Dutch-process cocoa (double-Dutch dark cocoa preferred) (22 grams)
¼ teaspoon baking soda
⅛ teaspoon fine sea salt
6 tablespoons (¾ stick) unsalted butter, room temperature (85 grams)
¼ cup granulated sugar (50 grams)
¼ cup packed light brown sugar (55 grams)
1 teaspoon pure vanilla extract
1 large egg yolk, room temperature

Filling
½ cup mascarpone or cream cheese, at room temperature (112 grams)
2½ tablespoons powdered sugar (20 grams)
2 tablespoons very finely chopped crystalized ginger

Baker's Note: For vanilla sugar, combine ½ cup granulated sugar (100 grams) and ½ vanilla bean, cut into 2 pieces, in a food processor. Pulse until vanilla bean is pulverized. Sieve mixture to remove any seeds.

Banana Bars

Makes 16 bars

Bring out your inner banana lover with these amazing taste-of-home, moist, and dense "banana-bread-in-cookie-form" bars. For the best texture, allow cookies to rest overnight, covered in the baking pan, before serving.

Preheat oven to 350°F/180°C/Gas Mark 4. Line an 8x8-inch baking pan with aluminum foil, leaving a 2-inch overhang on two opposite edges. Cut a piece of parchment to fit the bottom. Lightly oil the parchment and the sides of the pan.

In a medium bowl, sift together flours, baking powder, and salt. Set aside.

In the large bowl of an electric mixer, with speed set to high, beat together sour cream, butter, and sugar, about 2 minutes, until light and smooth. Add banana and vanilla. Beat about 1 minute to incorporate. Add egg. Beat 1 to 2 minutes, until combined. Set mixer speed to low. Gradually add flour mixture. Mix until well combined. Add chocolate chips and walnuts. Mix until just combined. Spoon evenly into prepared pan. Smooth top. Rest batter for 5 minutes before baking.

Bake for 25 to 30 minutes, until golden brown and firm to touch. Edges will be a shade darker and will be pulling away slightly from the sides. Remove from oven, place on a wire rack, and cool completely in the pan. When ready to serve, using the foil overhang, lift uncut bars from pan. Cut into 16 servings.

Store bars in an airtight container, at room temperature, for up to 3 days.

Spelt

Barley

INGREDIENTS

⅔ cup spelt flour (80 grams)
⅓ cup plus 2 tablespoons whole-grain barley flour (55 grams)
½ teaspoon baking powder
¼ teaspoon salt
¼ cup sour cream, room temperature (60 grams)
4 tablespoons (½ stick) unsalted butter, room temperature (57 grams)
¾ cup packed dark brown sugar (165 grams)
2 to 3 ripe bananas, peeled and mashed (about 1 cup) (262 grams)
1¼ teaspoons pure vanilla extract
1 large egg, room temperature
½ cup semisweet mini chocolate chips (82 grams)
⅓ cup whole walnuts, chopped (40 grams)

Spelt

Crunchy Cacao Nib Cookies

Chilling time: 2 hours or overnight
Makes about 36 cookies

Made with cacao nibs and the ancient grain spelt, these extra-dark, bittersweet, crunchy, triple-chocolate cookies are light and flavorful. The cacao nibs give them a crumbly crunch and a unique flavor. In testing these cookies, half of my taste testers liked the nibs in the batter and half preferred the cookies rolled in the nibs. It's all a matter of taste. If you want a crunchier texture, roll the cookies in the nibs rather than including them in the batter. If you want a mellower flavor, include the nibs in the batter, preparing the recipe as written. Use extra dark chocolate, such as Lindt 70% cacao chocolate bars, so the cookies are not too sweet.

In a medium bowl, sift together flour, baking powder, and salt. Set aside.

In the top of a double-boiler, over simmering water, melt butter and 2 ounces of chopped chocolate. Stir constantly until combined and thoroughly melted. Remove from heat, and cool for 5 minutes.

In the large bowl of an electric mixer, with speed set to high, beat the egg and sugar about 2 minutes, until light and fluffy. Set mixer speed to low. Add melted chocolate mixture. Mix until combined. Add vanilla. Mix until combined. Gradually add flour mixture. Mix until just incorporated. Add remaining 2 ounces of chopped chocolate and the cacao nibs (if including them in the batter). Stir until evenly distributed. Cover and chill for at least 2 hours or overnight.

Preheat oven to 350°F/180°C/Gas Mark 4. Line cookie sheets with parchment paper.

Using a small cookie scoop, such as #100, form 1¾ teaspoons of dough into ¾-inch balls. If you want the nibs on the outside of the cookies, roll the balls in the nibs. Place onto prepared sheets, spacing about 2 inches apart. Bake for 12 to 14 minutes, until firm to touch and tops are cracked. Transfer cookies, still on parchment, to wire racks to cool completely.

Store cookies in an airtight container, at room temperature, for up to 5 days.

INGREDIENTS

½ cup plus 2 tablespoons spelt flour (74 grams)
1 teaspoon baking powder
½ teaspoon fine kosher salt
4 tablespoons (½ stick) unsalted butter (57 grams)
4 ounces extra-dark, bittersweet chocolate (70% cacao), coarsely chopped, split into two portions (113 grams)
1 large egg, room temperature
½ cup plus 1 tablespoon granulated sugar (113 grams)
¾ teaspoon pure vanilla extract
¼ cup cacao nibs, for the batter or for rolling (34 grams)

Baker's Note: For a sweeter cookie, substitute 60% bittersweet chocolate for the extra-dark chocolate and omit the cacao nibs.

G-F

Hazelnut

Chocolate-Hazelnut Bars

Makes 16 bars

These flavorful, nutty, chocolate and hazelnut bar cookies got rave reviews from all of my testers. Loaded with hazelnuts, they are surprisingly tender, light, and chewy, with a moist crumb. Your gluten-free friends will appreciate this fancy, nut-flour treat that transports them to chocolate-hazelnut heaven.

Preheat the oven to 350°F/180°C/ Gas Mark 4. Line an 8x8 inch baking pan with aluminum foil, leaving a 2-inch overhang on two opposite edges. Cut a piece of parchment paper to fit the bottom. Lightly oil the parchment and the sides of the pan.

In a medium bowl, whisk together ground hazelnuts and baking powder. Set aside.

In the top of a double-boiler, over simmering water, melt unsweetened chocolate and butter. Stir constantly until chocolate and butter are fully combined and mixture is smooth. Set aside and cool about 5 minutes.

In the large bowl of an electric mixer, with speed set to high, beat eggs 2 to 3 minutes, until light and foamy. Add the sugars, vanilla, and salt. Beat 1 to 2 minutes, until light and fluffy. Reduce mixer speed to low. Add the melted chocolate mixture. Mix until combined. Add the flour mixture. Mix until combined. Add chopped hazelnuts and chocolate chips. Mix until just combined. Spoon evenly into prepared baking pan and smooth the top.

Bake for 25 to 30 minutes, until the top is firm to touch and the cookie is pulling away from the sides of the pan. The top should just begin to crack. Remove from oven, place on a cooling rack, and cool completely in the pan. When ready to serve, using the foil overhang, lift uncut bars from pan. Cut into 16 servings.

Store bars in an airtight container, at room temperature, for up to 3 days.

INGREDIENTS

¾ cup toasted hazelnuts, finely ground (86 grams)
½ teaspoon baking powder
3 ounces unsweetened chocolate (85 grams)
6 tablespoons (¾ stick) unsalted butter (85 grams)
2 large eggs, room temperature
½ cup packed light brown sugar (110 grams)
½ cup granulated sugar (100 grams)
1 teaspoon pure vanilla extract
⅛ teaspoon salt
½ cup toasted whole hazelnuts, coarsely chopped (58 grams)
½ cup semisweet chocolate chips (82 grams)

Baker's Note: For a sweeter cookie, substitute bittersweet or semisweet baking chocolate for the unsweetened chocolate. Do not use chocolate chips.

Five-Spice Ginger Cookies

Chilling time: 8 hours or overnight
Makes about 30 cookies

Chinese five-spice powder gives these moist, light, chewy cookies a balanced, gingery taste. They have a great mouthfeel and a mild, warm spice flavor that is not overbearing.

In a medium bowl, sift together flour, baking soda, salt, and spices. Set aside.

In the large bowl of an electric mixer, with speed set to high, combine the sugars and melted butter. Beat about 2 minutes, until combined. Add the egg. Beat about 2 minutes. Reduce mixer speed to low. Gradually add the flour mixture. Mix until combined. Cover and chill for at least 8 hours or overnight, for flavors to develop.

Preheat oven to 350°F/180°C/ Gas Mark 4. Line cookie sheets with parchment paper.

Using a small cookie scoop, such as #100, form 1¾ teaspoons of dough into ¾-inch balls. If desired, dip tops in raw sugar. Place on cookie sheets, spacing about 2 inches apart. Bake for 8 to 10 minutes, until golden brown. Cool for 5 minutes on cookie sheets. Transfer cookies, still on parchment, to wire racks to cool completely.

Store cookies in an airtight container, at room temperature, for up to 1 week.

INGREDIENTS

1 cup spelt flour (120 grams)
½ teaspoon baking soda
¼ teaspoon salt
1 teaspoon Chinese five-spice powder
½ teaspoon ground ginger
¼ cup packed light brown sugar (55 grams)
1½ tablespoons granulated sugar (25 grams)
8 tablespoons (1 stick) unsalted butter, melted and cooled (113 grams)
1 large egg, room temperature
Raw sugar, such as turbindo, for rolling (optional)

Spelt

Rye

Chocolate Brownies with Decadent Ganache Glaze

Makes 16 brownies

You will find that these delicious brownies are moist, with a complex and deeply chocolate taste. The complex flavor palate comes from the distinctive notes of the dark rye flour. Don't omit the chocolate ganache glaze, which adds a delicious dimension to the cakey brownie.

Preheat oven to 350°F/180°C/Gas Mark 4. Line an 8x8-inch baking pan with aluminum foil, leaving a 2-inch overhang on two opposite edges. Cut a piece of parchment to fit the bottom.

In a medium bowl, sift together flours, baking powder, and salt. Set aside.

In the top of a double-boiler, over simmering water, melt chocolate and butter. Stir until melted and smooth. Set aside, and cool for 5 minutes.

In the large bowl of an electric mixer, with speed set to high, beat sugar, eggs, and vanilla, about 3 minutes, until light and fluffy. With a rubber spatula, fold in melted chocolate mixture in 2 to 3 batches. Fold in flour mixture. Pour evenly into prepared pan. Smooth top.

Bake for 20 to 25 minutes, until surface begins to crack and pull away from the sides. Transfer pan to a wire rack and let cool for 1 to 1½ hours before glazing.

Place chopped chocolate in a small bowl. In a small saucepan, heat cream over low heat, until it simmers slightly. Remove from the heat and pour cream over chocolate. Stir until smooth and mixture just starts to thicken. Spoon over brownies. Let stand at room temperature until glaze is set, about 1 hour. When ready to serve, using foil overhang, lift uncut brownies from pan. Cut into 16 servings.

Store brownies in an airtight container, at room temperature, for up to 5 days.

INGREDIENTS

½ cup spelt flour (60 grams)
¼ cup whole-grain dark rye flour (30 grams)
½ teaspoon baking powder
½ teaspoon salt
6 ounces semisweet or bittersweet (60% cacao) chocolate, coarsely chopped (170 grams)
8 tablespoons (1 stick) unsalted butter (113 grams)
¾ cup granulated sugar (150 grams)
2 large eggs, room temperature
1 teaspoon pure vanilla extract

Ganache Glaze
4 ounces semisweet or bittersweet (60% cacao) chocolate, finely chopped (113 grams)
¼ cup plus 2 tablespoons heavy cream

Baker's Note: For the brownie base, you can use a mix of semisweet and bittersweet (60% cacao) chocolate, if you prefer a sweeter taste.

Pecan Sables

Chilling time: overnight
Makes about 50 cookies

These delightful pecan and rye-flour cookies, reminiscent of pecan balls or Mexican wedding cakes, are very fragrant and mildly sweet. The powdered sugar dusting gives them a lovely finish. You can find organic, whole-grain dark rye flour, such as Bob's Red Mill, in the specialty flour section of most supermarkets.

In the bowl of a food processor, combine toasted pecans, flour, sugar, salt, and vanilla. Pulse until very finely ground, about 1 minute. Mixture will resemble sand. Transfer to a large bowl. Drop butter onto flour mixture. With a pastry cutter, cut in butter until mixture resembles coarse meal and begins to form a rough dough. The mixture will be dry and sandy, but don't worry. Gather together with your hands and lightly knead into a cohesive mass. Cover and chill overnight, for flours to hydrate.

Preheat the oven to 350°F/180°C/ Gas Mark 4. Line cookie sheets with parchment paper.

Using a small cookie scoop, such as #100, form 1¾ teaspoons of dough into ¾-inch balls. Place on prepared sheets, spacing about 1 inch apart. Bake for 10 to 12 minutes, until golden brown around the edges. Cool for 1 minute on cookie sheets. Transfer cookies, still on parchment, to wire racks. Cool for 5 more minutes. Dust cookies with powdered sugar. Cool completely. If desired, just before serving, dust again with powdered sugar or coat completely by rolling in powdered sugar.

Store cookies in an airtight container, at room temperature, for up to one week.

INGREDIENTS

1⅔ cups toasted pecans (186 grams)
1½ cups whole-grain dark rye flour (186 grams)
⅔ cup granulated sugar (133 grams)
¼ teaspoon fine sea salt
1½ teaspoons pure vanilla extract
9 tablespoons (1⅛ stick) unsalted butter, room temperature, cut into ¼-inch cubes (127 grams)
Powdered sugar, for dusting

Baker's Note: Toast pecans at 350°F/180°C/ Gas Mark 4 for 5 minutes. Cool before using. Cookies will harden as they cool, so don't overbake.

Baby Raisin Cookies

Chilling time: overnight
Makes about 60 cookies

Zante currants (dried baby raisins) are the essential ingredient in these well-balanced, soft cookies. My testers liked these cookies best rolled in sugar or iced with yummy brown butter frosting. In fact, one taste tester thought anything this scrumptious should be illegal.

In a medium bowl, sift together flours, baking powder, salt, and cinnamon. Set aside.

In the large bowl of an electric mixer, with speed set to high, beat butter and sugar 1 to 2 minutes, until light and fluffy. Add egg and vanilla. Beat about 1 minute, until fluffy. Reduce mixer speed to low. Gradually add the flour mixture. Mix until just incorporated. Add currants and walnuts. Mix until just combined. Cover and chill overnight, for flours to hydrate and flavors to meld.

Preheat oven to 350°F/180°C/Gas Mark 4. Line cookie sheets with parchment paper.

Using a small cookie scoop, such as #100, form 1¾ teaspoons of dough into ¾-inch balls. If desired, dip tops of cookies in sugar (or frost with icing after baking). Place on prepared cookie sheets, spacing about 1 inch apart, and flatten to ⅓-inch thickness. Bake for 8 to 12 minutes, until edges are golden brown. Cool for 2 minutes on cookie sheets. Transfer cookies, still on parchment, to wire racks to cool completely.

In a small saucepan, over low heat, melt butter and heat until it foams. Cook for 1 minute or less, until the foam begins to turn golden along the edges and you see small brown bits forming. Watch carefully, as butter browns quickly and can become scorched if heated too long. Immediately remove from heat, and stir in powdered sugar. Add just enough cream to make icing the desired consistency for spreading. Using a small off-set spatula or a knife, coat tops of cookies with icing, or place icing in a pastry bag and decorate cookies. Place cookies on racks for icing to dry.

Store iced cookies in an airtight container, at room temperature, between layers of wax paper or parchment, for up to 3 days. Layering between papers is not necessary for cookies that are not iced.

INGREDIENTS

¾ cup kamut flour (90 grams)
¾ cup spelt flour (90 grams)
½ teaspoon baking powder
½ teaspoon salt
¼ teaspoon cinnamon
12 tablespoons (1½ sticks) unsalted butter, room temperature (170 grams)
⅔ cup granulated sugar (133 grams)
1 large egg, room temperature
1 teaspoon pure vanilla extract
½ cup dried Zante currants (80 grams)
½ cup toasted whole walnuts, finely chopped (59 grams)
Extra granulated sugar, for rolling (optional)

Brown Butter Icing (Optional)
2 tablespoons (¼ stick) unsalted butter (14 grams)
1½ cups powdered sugar (188 grams)
3 to 4 tablespoons heavy cream, room temperature

Baker's Note: Toast walnuts for 5 minutes at 350°F/180°C/Gas Mark 4, to bring out their full flavor.

Chocolate-Hazelnut Meringues

Makes about 40 cookies

These distinctive chocolate-hazelnut cookies are crunchy, light, and chewy, with a powdery, sweet, and nutty taste. They are delicious with a dish of dark chocolate ice cream.

Preheat oven to 275°F/140°C/ Gas Mark 1. Line cookie sheets with parchment paper.

In the small bowl of an electric mixer, with speed set to high, beat egg whites about 2 minutes, until foamy and soft peaks form. Add cream of tartar and salt. Beat until incorporated. Add sugar, one tablespoon at a time. Beat 2 to 3 minutes, until stiff peaks form. Add vanilla. Beat until mixed in completely. Using a rubber spatula, carefully fold in hazelnuts and chocolate, in 2 or 3 batches, being careful not to deflate the batter.

Place 2 teaspoons of batter onto prepared cookie sheets, spacing about 2 inches apart. Smooth out any peaks. Bake for 25 to 30 minutes, until lightly browned and firm to touch. Remove from oven. Place cookie sheets on wire racks to cool completely.

Store cookies in an airtight container, at room temperature, for up to 5 days.

INGREDIENTS

2 large egg whites, room temperature
$\frac{1}{16}$ teaspoon cream of tartar
$\frac{1}{16}$ teaspoon salt
$\frac{2}{3}$ cup superfine sugar (133 grams)
$\frac{1}{8}$ teaspoon pure vanilla extract
1$\frac{1}{3}$ cups toasted whole hazelnuts, chopped
   (153 grams)
2 ounces bittersweet or semisweet
   chocolate, finely chopped (57 grams)

Baker's Note: Rinse mixing bowl with warm water and dry thoroughly before beating the eggs. The warmth from the bowl will help the eggs form peaks faster. If you wish, you can use a #60 scoop to place the batter on the cookie sheets.

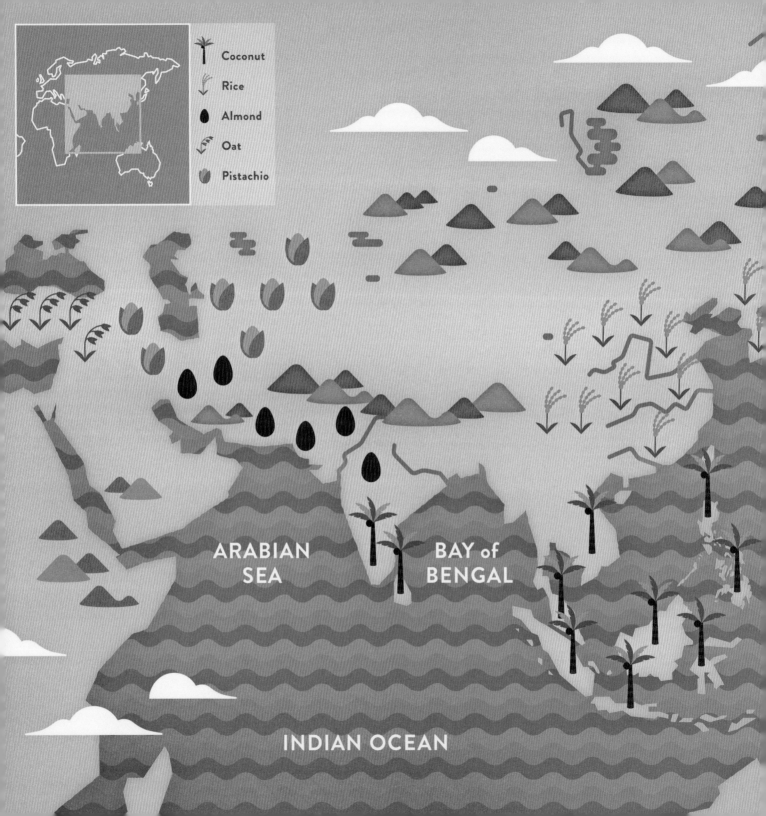

Coconut
Rice
Almond
Oat
Pistachio

ARABIAN
SEA

BAY of
BENGAL

INDIAN OCEAN

Asia and the Pacific Basin

Asia and the Pacific Basin, a huge geographic area, are home to many of today's domesticated food sources, including rice, oats, coconuts, almonds, and pistachios.

Myths about ancient farming in China focus on the "Five Grains," or five cereals that sustain life and hence civilization. Lists of the Five Grains, dating back to about 2700 BC, vary considerably. Some include oats and rice, as well as millet, soy, wheat, barley, sesame, and adzuki bean.

Regardless of what the actual Five Grains were, rice cultivation marks the development of agriculture in China. In fact, Chinese legends attribute the domestication of rice to Shennong, the legendary Emperor of China who is considered the inventor of Chinese agriculture. Evidence of early agriculture in China has been found along the Yellow, Yangtze, and Pearl Rivers, dating back some 8,200 to 13,500 years.

Oats and several nut varieties used in baking and confections are also native to Asia. Oats, with a murky lineage, are believed to have originated in Asia Minor, as is my favorite nut, the pistachio. The almond is native to Asia, and the coconut was brought under cultivation in the Pacific Basin and the Indian Ocean Basin. Unlike wheat and its relatives, all of these flours are gluten-free.

The recipes in this chapter contain flours made from oats, brown rice, coconut, almonds, and pistachios.

Top row: Steel-cut oatmeal, brown-rice flour; middle row: pistachio flour, almond flour, old-fashioned oatmeal; bottom row: coconut flour, oat flour

Oatmeal (Old-Fashioned and Steel-Cut)

The history of oats is somewhat murky. Some believe they originated in Asia Minor. Others believe they originated in central Asia. They grow well in cool, moist climates and have been used as food for livestock and humans since ancient times. They are believed to be the last of the cereal crops to have been domesticated. The oldest known cultivated oats were found in Switzerland, dating back to the Bronze Age of 1700 BC to 500 BC.

Oats are gluten-free. They have a nutty, slightly sweet flavor and impart a chewy texture to baked goods. Oats have a soluble fiber that scientific studies have found to lower blood serum cholesterol. Due to this health benefit, the demand for oats has steadily increased over the last ten to fifteen years.

Oatmeal is a common form of oats used in baking. Old-fashioned rolled oats are steamed oat groats (husked whole oat kernels) that have been flattened by a roller. Quick-cooking oats are a form of rolled oats in which the grain is cut into pieces before steaming and rolling, creating smaller oat flakes. Both can be used interchangeably in cookie recipes. However, the result is a somewhat different texture and chew.

Steel-cut oats, also called pin-head oats, are groats that have been cut into two or three pieces. They are often used in porridge. They are used sparingly in baking as they are hard and make cookie textures chewier.

Oat Flour

Oat flour is made from grinding oat grouts into a powder. It is a bit denser than wheat flour, so it is best used in combination with nut butters or other flours. You can buy oat flour from specialty flour producers, like Bob's Red Mill, or you can make it yourself by grinding rolled oats into a fine powder using a food processer or a blender.

Brown-Rice Flour

Rice has been a food staple for thousands of years, originating in China some 8,200 to 13,500 years ago and spreading to Southeast Asia, Europe, and eventually to the Americas. Today, rice feeds over half of the world's population. Rice flour is made from finely milled rice and may be made from either white or brown rice.

Brown-rice flour is gluten-free and milled from whole-grain brown rice. It has a mild, nutty flavor and a chewier texture than its white counterpart. It is a good substitute for wheat flour and is used extensively in gluten-free baking, often in combination with other flours. To avoid a gritty texture, use very finely milled rice flour from King Arthur Flour or Bob's Red Mill.

Almond Flour

Almonds, which are referred to as nuts, are technically drupes, or a type of fruit. They are believed to have originated in southeast or western Asia. They eventually spread throughout the Mediterranean and Europe, where they were frequently used in cooking. In the USA, almond production is concentrated in California, which produces 80 percent of the world's almonds and 100 percent of the USA's commercial supply.

Almond flour is made from ground blanched almonds. Almond meal is made from ground almonds that have retained their skins. Both are readily available in supermarkets, or if you are so inclined, you can make your own by grinding nuts in a food processer or nut chopper. Almond flour and meal are suitable for people with gluten-free diets or celiac disease. The recipes in this book call for almond flour, not meal.

Pistachios

My favorite nut, the pistachio, originated in western Asia or

Asia Minor around 6700 BC. A member of the cashew family, it is technically a drupe, not a nut.

Pistachios thrive in dry climates. In the USA, pistachios are grown in California. In fact, the USA is the largest global producer of pistachios.

Historically, pistachios are eaten whole or are used in a variety of prepared foods such as ice cream, confections, and baked goods. The recipes in this book call for finely chopped or ground unsalted pistachios, which are used in combination with other nut flours or whole-grain flours.

Coconut Flour

The coconut, a member of the palm family, is also botanically a drupe, not a nut. It is a versatile plant with many different uses.

According to research conducted in 2011, the coconut was brought under cultivation thousands of years ago, in two separate locations. The first was in the Pacific Basin, most likely on islands in southeast Asia, specifically the Philippines, Malaysia, and Indonesia. The other early cultivation location was in the Indian Ocean Basin along the southern periphery of India, most likely what is now Sri Lanka, the Maldives, and the Laccadives. Today, coconut palms are grown in more than ninety countries. Most of the commercial coconut products are from Indonesia, the Philippines, and India.

Coconut flour is made from ground coconut meat. It has the highest fiber content of any flour. It also has a high fat content and should be stored in the freezer to keep it fresh. Because of its high fiber content, it absorbs more liquids than other flours. Baked goods made of coconut flour can fall apart easily, so binding them with eggs and adding sufficient liquid are important.

Many recipes in this chapter include coconut flour, dried coconut, or coconut milk.

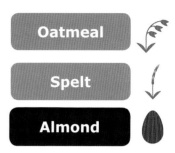

Oatmeal

Spelt

Almond

Coconut Oatmeal Lace

Chilling time: 4 hours or overnight
Makes about 60 cookies

When I first made these cookies, I included chocolate chips in the recipe. However, I found that the recipe is great with just oats, almonds, and coconut. My testers call these crispy, lacy cookies "crunchtastic." Be sure to toast the almonds and chill the dough overnight to hydrate the oats. They are hands-down great!

In a medium bowl, whisk together oats, flours, baking powder, baking soda, and salt. Set aside.

In the large bowl of an electric mixer, with speed set to high, beat the butter and sugars 1 to 2 minutes, until light and creamy. Add the egg. Beat 1 to 2 minutes, until fluffy. Add milk and extracts. Beat until thoroughly incorporated. Set the mixer speed to low. Gradually add the flour mixture and mix until just incorporated. Add almonds and coconut. Mix until just combined. Chill 4 hours or overnight, to hydrate the oats.

Preheat oven to 350°F/180°C/Gas Mark 4. Line cookie sheets with parchment paper.

Using a small cookie scoop, such as #100, form 1¾ teaspoons of dough into ¾-inch balls. Place on prepared sheets, spacing about 2½ inches apart. Don't crowd the cookies, as they will spread considerably while baking. Bake for 8 to 10 minutes, until golden brown. Monitor them carefully in the final 1 to 2 minutes, as they will crisp quickly. Cool for 1 minute on cookie sheets. Transfer cookies, still on parchment, to wire racks to cool completely.

Store cookies in an airtight container, at room temperature, between layers of wax paper or parchment, for up to 1 week.

INGREDIENTS

¾ cup old-fashioned rolled oats (68 grams)
½ cup spelt flour (60 grams)
¼ cup almond flour (28 grams)
½ teaspoon baking powder
½ teaspoon baking soda
½ teaspoon sea salt
8 tablespoons (1 stick) unsalted butter, room temperature (113 grams)
½ cup granulated sugar (100 grams)
½ cup packed dark brown sugar (110 grams)
1 large egg, room temperature
1 tablespoon whole milk
1 teaspoon pure vanilla extract
½ teaspoon pure almond extract
⅓ cup toasted whole almonds, chopped (53 grams)
⅓ cup shredded sweetened coconut, coarsely chopped (40 grams)

Baker's Note: In a 350°F/180°C/Gas Mark 4 oven, toast almonds 5 to 7 minutes, until fragrant.

Whole Wheat

Oatmeal

Apple Bars with Streusel Topping

Makes 16 bars

My husband says that these homey, light, flaky, sweet bars are like a little piece of apple pie in a bar. To make these yummy bars, thinly slice tart apples such as Granny Smith, Macintosh, or Fuji and arrange the slices over the crust. The thinner the slices, the better. I like to use mace, a relative to nutmeg, in my bars as the flavor reminds me of my grandma's apple pie. For a delicious treat, serve these cookies with a scoop of dulce de leche ice cream.

Preheat oven to 350°F/180°C/Gas Mark 4. Line an 8x8 inch baking pan with aluminum foil, leaving a 2-inch overhang on two opposite edges. Cut a piece of parchment paper to fit the bottom of the pan. Place parchment on top of foil. Lightly oil the parchment and the sides of the pan.

In the bowl of a food processor, combine 1 cup of flour, oats, brown sugar, and salt. Pulse 20 to 30 seconds. Add butter and water. Pulse about 1 minute, until the dough begins to gather together and sticks together when pressed. Divide the dough mixture in half. Using a rubber spatula, press half of the dough evenly in the bottom of prepared pan. Using a fork, stir sliced almonds into the remaining dough. Set aside.

In a medium bowl, combine apples, sugar, ½ tablespoon of flour, and spices. With a large spoon, stir, thoroughly coating the apples with the sugar mixture. Arrange the apple slices evenly over the dough. Spread any sugary juices left in the bowl over the apple slices. With your fingers, sprinkle the remaining dough evenly on top of the apples, covering apple slices completely. Using a rubber spatula, press down firmly but gently. Bake for 35 to 40 minutes, until golden brown. Place on wire rack and cool completely in the pan. When ready to serve, using the foil overhang, lift the uncut bars from pan. Cut into 16 servings. Serve immediately.

Store bars in an airtight container, at room temperature or in the refrigerator, for up to 3 days.

INGREDIENTS

1 cup white whole-wheat flour (130 grams)
1 cup old-fashioned rolled oats (90 grams)
¼ cup packed light brown sugar (55 grams)
¼ teaspoon salt
8 tablespoons (1 stick) unsalted butter, cold, cut into ¼-inch cubes (113 grams)
1 tablespoon cold water
2 tablespoons sliced almonds (14 grams)
2 large tart apples, peeled and sliced into ⅛- to ¼-inch thick slices (about 3 cups)
¼ cup granulated sugar (50 grams)
½ tablespoon white whole-wheat flour
½ teaspoon ground cinnamon, preferably ground roasted cinnamon
⅛ teaspoon ground mace, optional

Baker's Note: If you prefer a smooth top, omit the sliced almonds from the topping.

Winter-Sun Oat Cookies

Chilling time: overnight
Makes about 15 cookies

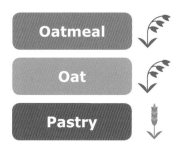

Oatmeal

Oat

Pastry

INGREDIENTS

1 cup old-fashioned rolled oats (90 grams)
⅓ cup oat flour (40 grams)
¼ cup whole-wheat pastry flour (33 grams)
¼ teaspoon baking soda
¼ teaspoon baking powder
¼ teaspoon salt
¼ teaspoon ground cinnamon, preferably
  ground roasted cinnamon
6 tablespoons (¾ stick) unsalted butter, room
  temperature (85 grams)
⅓ cup packed dark brown sugar (73 grams)
¾ teaspoon pure vanilla extract

Baker's Note: If you are not a cinnamon fan,
you can omit the cinnamon. The resulting
cookie will still have a complex flavor but a less
interesting finish.

I have read that in medieval times, the Scottish people made cookies in the shape of the sun, from oats and butter, to celebrate the winter solstice. I thought I would create my own modern version with brown sugar and warm, roasted cinnamon. My sweet and delicious adaptation uses oat flour, oatmeal, and whole-wheat pastry flour. Its complex flavor is light and buttery, and it has a pleasant, chewy texture.

In a medium bowl, whisk together oats, flours, baking soda, baking powder, salt, and cinnamon. Set aside.

In the large bowl of an electric mixer, with speed set to high, beat the butter, sugar, and vanilla for 1 to 2 minutes, until light and fluffy. Reduce mixer speed to low. Gradually add flour mixture. Mix until just combined and dough has begun to form clumps. Gather together with hands. Cover and chill overnight, for flours to hydrate.

Preheat oven to 350°F/180°C/ Gas Mark 4. Line cookie sheets with parchment paper.

Using a medium cookie scoop, such as #60, form 2 teaspoons of dough into 1-inch balls. Place on prepared sheets, spacing about 2½ inches apart. Flatten to ⅓-inch thickness. Bake for 12 to 14 minutes, until light brown. Cool for 2 minutes on cookie sheets. Transfer cookies, still on parchment, to wire racks to cool completely.

Store cookies in an airtight container, at room temperature, for up to 1 week.

Coconut

Coconut Fudge Brownies

Makes 16 brownies

These deeply chocolate, moist, rich brownies made with unsweetened coconut, coconut milk, and coconut flour are perfect. If I had to pick one cookie as my favorite, this would be it. Plus, they are gluten-free! Coconut flour absorbs a lot of moisture, so weigh or measure carefully and don't omit the coconut milk.

Preheat the oven to 350°F/180°C/ Gas Mark 4. Line an 8x8-inch baking pan with aluminum foil, leaving a 2-inch overhang on two opposite edges. Cut a piece of parchment paper to fit the bottom. Lightly oil the parchment and the sides of the pan.

In a medium bowl, whisk together flour, baking powder, and salt. Set aside.

In the top of a double-boiler, over simmering water, melt unsweetened chocolate and butter. Stir constantly, until chocolate and butter are fully combined and mixture is smooth. Set aside and cool about 5 minutes.

In the large bowl of an electric mixer, with speed set to high, beat eggs for 2 to 3 minutes, until light and foamy. Add sugar, coconut milk, and vanilla. Beat 1 to 2 minutes, until light and fluffy. Reduce mixer speed to low. Add chocolate mixture. Mix until combined. Add flour mixture. Mix until combined. Add coconut and chocolate chips. Mix until just combined.

Spoon the batter evenly into prepared pan. Smooth the top. Bake for 20 to 25 minutes, until the top is firm to touch and faintly cracked. It will pull away from the sides of the pan just slightly. Don't overbake. Place on wire rack and cool completely in the pan. When ready to serve, using the foil overhang, lift uncut bars from pan. Cut into 16 servings.

Store brownies in an airtight container, at room temperature or in the refrigerator, for up to 5 days.

INGREDIENTS

¾ cup coconut flour (84 grams)
½ teaspoon baking powder
⅛ teaspoon salt
3 ounces unsweetened chocolate (85 grams)
8 tablespoons (1 stick) unsalted butter (113 grams)
3 large eggs, room temperature
1 cup granulated sugar (200 grams)
¼ cup stirred unsweetened coconut milk, room temperature
1 teaspoon pure vanilla extract
½ cup shredded unsweetened coconut, coarsely chopped (40 grams)
¾ cup bittersweet (60% cacao) chocolate chips (122 grams)

Baker's Note: For a sweeter cookie, use semisweet chocolate chips.

Cashew-Oatmeal Cookies

Makes about 20 cookies

This easy-to-make cookie, made with creamy cashew butter and steel-cut oats, is light, nutty, and slightly chewy. It is great for an afternoon snack or a lunch box dessert. Some folks have even teamed it with a little tart jam to make the perfect breakfast cookie. Breakfast, lunch, or snack, it's up to you! If you don't have steel-cut oats, you can substitute old-fashioned rolled oats, for a slightly less chewy cookie.

Preheat oven to 350°F/180°C/Gas Mark 4. Line cookie sheets with parchment paper.

If oil has separated from cashew butter, stir until all oil is mixed in and it has a smooth consistency.

In the bowl of a small food processor, pulse the steel-cut oats 1 minute or less, until coarsely ground. If using rolled oats, do not grind in a food processer. Set aside.

In a large bowl, whisk together sugar, baking soda, and salt. Add cashew butter. In a small bowl, beat egg with a whisk or fork, until it has increased 3 times in volume. Add beaten egg to cashew-butter mixture. Using a large spoon, stir until combined. Stir in oats. Let sit for 10 minutes, uncovered, at room temperature.

Using a medium cookie scoop, such as #50, form 1 tablespoon of dough into 1¼-inch balls. Place on prepared sheets, spacing about 2 inches apart. Flatten to ½-inch thickness. Bake for 12 to 14 minutes, until golden brown. Cool for 2 minutes on cookie sheets. Transfer cookies, still on parchment, to wire racks to cool completely.

Store cookies in an airtight container, at room temperature, for up to 1 week.

INGREDIENTS

1 cup unsalted, creamy cashew butter, room temperature (240 grams)

3 tablespoons steel-cut oats (29 grams) or 3 tablespoons old-fashioned rolled oats (18 grams)

¾ cup granulated sugar (150 grams)

½ teaspoon baking soda

¼ teaspoon fine sea salt

1 large egg, room temperature

G-F

Almond

Hazelnut

Almond-Hazelnut Cookies

Makes about 24 cookies

You will love the slightly sweet and nutty taste of almonds and hazelnuts in these light, chewy, macaroon-like cookies. They are adapted from a recipe that was handed down from my mom and grandma. Make them plain, or sprinkle with granulated sugar.

Preheat oven to 300°F/150°C/Gas Mark 2. Line cookie sheets with parchment paper.

In the small bowl of an electric mixer, with speed set to medium, beat egg yolk 1 to 2 minutes, until pale yellow. Gradually add sugar and beat until combined. Add salt and vanilla. Beat until combined. Set mixer speed to low. Add ground nuts. Mix until thoroughly combined. Transfer mixture to another bowl. Set aside.

Clean bowl and blades of the electric mixer.

In the small bowl of the electric mixer, with speed set to high, beat egg white until foamy. Add cream of tartar. Beat about 2 minutes, until soft peaks form. Using a rubber spatula, carefully fold in nut mixture, in 2 or 3 batches.

Using a small cookie scoop, such as #100, form 1¾ teaspoons of dough into ¾-inch balls. Place on prepared sheets, spacing about 2 inches apart. Sprinkle with granulated sugar, if desired. Bake for 15 to 20 minutes, until pale golden brown and edges are a shade darker. Transfer cookies, still on parchment, to wire racks to cool completely.

Store cookies in an airtight container, at room temperature, for up to one week.

INGREDIENTS

1 large egg, separated
½ cup granulated sugar (100 grams)
¼ teaspoon salt
¼ teaspoon pure vanilla extract
¼ cup plus 2 tablespoons toasted whole almonds, finely ground (60 grams)
¼ cup plus 2 tablespoons toasted whole hazelnuts, finely ground (45 grams)
¼ teaspoon cream of tartar
3 tablespoons granulated sugar for sprinkling, optional (38 grams)

Baker's Note: Toasting the hazelnuts and almonds at 350°F/180°C/Gas Mark 4 for 5 to 7 minutes brings out a deep, nutty flavor.

Chocolate-Oatmeal-Walnut Cookies

Chilling time: 4 hours or overnight
Makes about 36 cookies

To repay the generosity of an old friend for sending me a very special baking book, I made him these chocolate-oatmeal-walnut cookies. I toast the walnuts for a deep, nutty flavor and chill the dough overnight to hydrate the oats. These cookies are moist, chewy, and absolutely scrumptious! They will make the oatmeal cookie lovers in your life very happy.

In a medium bowl, whisk together flour, oats, baking powder, baking soda, and salt. Set aside.

In the large bowl of an electric mixer, with speed set to high, beat butter and sugar about 2 minutes, until light and fluffy. Add molasses. Beat until combined. Add egg. Beat 1 to 2 minutes, until light and fluffy. Add milk and vanilla. Beat until thoroughly combined. Set mixer speed to low. Gradually add flour mixture until just incorporated. Add chocolate chips and walnuts. Mix until just combined. Chill for 4 hours or overnight, to hydrate the oats.

Preheat oven to 350°F/180°C/ Gas Mark 4. Line cookie sheets with parchment paper.

Using a medium cookie scoop, such as #50, form 1 tablespoon of dough into 1¼-inch balls. Place on prepared sheets, spacing about 2½ inches apart. Flatten to ⅓- to ¼-inch thickness. Bake for 10 to 14 minutes, until golden brown. Cool for 2 minutes on cookie sheets. Transfer cookies, still on parchment, to wire racks to cool completely.

Store cookies in an airtight container, at room temperature, for up to 1 week.

INGREDIENTS

1 cup white whole-wheat flour (130 grams)
1 cup old-fashioned rolled oats (90 grams)
½ teaspoon baking powder
½ teaspoon baking soda
½ teaspoon fine sea salt
8 tablespoons (1 stick) unsalted butter, room temperature (113 grams)
¾ cup plus 2 tablespoons granulated sugar (175 grams)
2 tablespoons molasses
1 large egg, room temperature
1 tablespoon whole milk
1½ teaspoons pure vanilla extract
1 cup bittersweet (60% cacao) chocolate chips (163 grams)
½ cup toasted walnuts, coarsely chopped (59 grams)

Baker's Note: Toast walnuts 5 to 7 minutes, at 350°F/180°C/Gas Mark 4, until fragrant.

Tropical Lime-Coconut Cookies

Chilling time: 2 hours or overnight
Makes about 30 cookies

Coconut flour adds a deep coconut taste to these chewy cookies, perfumed with lime and unsweetened coconut. They are a great snack or accompaniment to vanilla ice cream. Coconut flour is very absorbent and fiber-rich, so don't leave out the milk.

In a medium bowl, sift together flours, baking soda, and salt. Set aside.

In the large bowl of an electric mixer, with speed set to high, beat butter and sugars for 1 to 2 minutes, until light and fluffy. Add egg. Beat 1 to 2 minutes, until fluffy. Add milk and zest. Mix until incorporated. Set mixer speed to low. Gradually add flour mixture, mixing thoroughly. Add chocolate morsels and coconut.

Mix until just combined. Cover and chill for 2 hours or overnight.

Preheat oven to 350°F/180°C/ Gas Mark 4. Line cookie sheets with parchment paper.

Using a medium scoop, such as #50, form 1 tablespoon of dough into 1¼-inch balls. Place on cookie sheets, spacing 2½ inches apart. Do not crowd cookies, as they spread considerably while baking. Bake for 10 to 12 minutes, until golden brown on the edges. Cool for 5 minutes on cookie sheets. Transfer cookies, still on parchment, to wire racks to cool completely. They will crisp as they cool.

Store cookies in an airtight container, at room temperature, for up to 5 days.

INGREDIENTS

¾ cup spelt flour (90 grams)
¼ cup coconut flour (28 grams)
½ teaspoon baking soda
¼ teaspoon fine sea salt
8 tablespoons (1 stick) unsalted butter, room temperature (113 grams)
½ cup granulated sugar (100 grams)
¼ cup packed light brown sugar (55 grams)
1 large egg, room temperature
2 tablespoons whole milk
1½ teaspoons packed, finely chopped or grated lime zest
¾ cup premium white chocolate morsels, coarsely chopped (117 grams)
½ cup unsweetened coconut, finely chopped (40 grams)

G-F

Oatmeal

Bird Bars

Makes 16 bars

Inspired by various recipes and commercially available granola bars, I created my own seed-cookie-granola-bar. Judging from the praise my creation received from lovers of high-end granola bars, I succeeded admirably. This colorful, flavorful bar, made with roasted ground cinnamon for a deep cinnamon flavor, is sweet and chewy and has what taste testers described as "unique notes and a satisfying texture." Be prepared to hear, "This is the best granola bar I've ever eaten!" Be sure to use gluten-free rolled oats if serving these cookies to people with celiac disease or gluten intolerance.

Preheat oven to 350°F/180°C/ Gas Mark 4. Line an 8x8-inch square baking pan with aluminum foil, leaving a 2-inch overhang on two opposite edges. Cut a piece of parchment paper to fit bottom of pan. Lightly oil the parchment and the sides of the pan. Set aside.

In a medium bowl, mix together oats, almonds, cranberries, seeds, cinnamon, and salt. Set aside.

In a large saucepan, over low heat, melt butter, honey, and sugar. Stir constantly. Bring to a boil and stir until sugar has dissolved completely. Remove from heat. Stir in oat mixture. Spoon evenly into prepared pan and press down with back of spoon. Smooth top. Bake for 15 to 20 minutes, until top is golden. Place on wire rack and cool completely in the pan. When ready to serve, using the foil overhang, lift uncut bars from pan. If there are any droplets of liquefied butter and sugar on the bottom of the uncut bar, gently blot with a paper towel. Cut into 16 servings.

Store bars in an airtight container, at room temperature, for up to 5 days.

INGREDIENTS

1¼ cups gluten-free, old-fashioned rolled oats (113 grams)

½ scant cup whole almonds, coarsely chopped (70 grams)

⅔ cup dried cranberries (80 grams)

3 tablespoons shelled, unsalted, raw pumpkin seeds (a.k.a. pepitas)

3 tablespoons shelled, unsalted, raw sunflower seeds

2 tablespoons white or black sesame seeds

¾ teaspoon ground cinnamon, preferably ground roasted cinnamon

⅛ teaspoon fine sea salt

5½ tablespoons (⅔ stick) unsalted butter (78 grams)

¼ cup organic honey (68 grams)

½ cup raw sugar, such as turbindo (100 grams)

Baker's Note: To make a more decadent treat, add a scant ½ cup (80 grams) of semisweet mini chocolate chips to the oat-nut-fruit mixture.

Coconut Shortbread Cookies

Chilling time: 2 hours or overnight

Makes 50 small or 30 medium unfilled cookies, or 25 small or 15 medium filled sandwich cookies

Coconut flour adds a mild toasted-coconut flavor to these slightly chewy but tender cookies, and the lemon brightens the coconut flavor. My taste testers could not agree on their favorite, so you might want to try them plain, with lemon glaze, or, if you are a lemon fiend like me, sandwiched with my zesty lemon curd-mascarpone filling. I use Boyajian lemon oil in the glaze, but you can substitute lemon extract and zest to achieve a similar flavor.

In a medium bowl, sift together flours, powdered sugar, and salt. Drop butter onto flour mixture. With a pastry cutter, cut in butter until it resembles coarse meal. Using a fork, stir in coconut. Mix in vanilla and cream. Stir until the dough comes together, and shape into a disk. Wrap in wax paper or plastic wrap. Chill for 2 hours or overnight, for flours to hydrate.

Preheat oven to 350°F/180°C/ Gas Mark 4. Line cookie sheets with parchment paper.

Roll dough between sheets of wax paper to ¼-inch thickness and cut with 1-inch or 1½-inch round cookie cutter. Place on prepared sheets, spacing 1 inch apart. Bake for 8 to 10 minutes, until edges are golden brown. Cool for 2 minutes on cookie sheets. Transfer cookies, still on parchment, to wire racks to cool completely.

If topping with glaze, wait until cookies have cooled. In a small bowl, combine all glaze ingredients and mix with a spoon until smooth. Using a pastry brush, brush the top of each cookie with glaze. Allow glaze to dry before serving or storing.

If making a sandwich cookie, wait to prepare filling until ready to serve cookies. Combine all filling ingredients in a small bowl. With a large spoon, mix together until well combined. Spread ½ teaspoon of the filling over flat side of half of the cookies. Sandwich with another cookie. Serve filled cookies immediately.

Store unfilled cookies in an airtight container, at room temperature, for up to 5 days.

INGREDIENTS

¾ cup spelt flour (90 grams)
¼ cup coconut flour (29 grams)
⅓ cup powdered sugar (42 grams)
¼ teaspoon salt
8 tablespoons (1 stick) unsalted butter, cold, cut into ¼-inch cubes (113 grams)
½ cup unsweetened coconut, finely chopped (40 grams)
½ teaspoon pure vanilla extract
1 tablespoon heavy cream

Glaze

½ cup powdered sugar, sifted (63 grams)
⅛ teaspoon lemon oil (or substitute ¼ teaspoon pure lemon extract plus ¼ teaspoon packed, finely chopped or grated lemon zest)
1½ tablespoons boiling water

Filling

½ cup lemon curd, room temperature (152 grams)
2 tablespoons mascarpone cheese (or substitute cream cheese), room temperature (28 grams)
½ teaspoon packed, finely chopped or grated lemon zest

Baker's Note: If dough is chilled overnight, let it stand about 2 to 3 minutes prior to rolling so that it is pliable.

G-F

Pistachio

Rice

Pistachio Drops

Chilling time: overnight
Makes about 55 cookies

These yummy, gluten-free cookies are made with a delicious fifty-fifty grain and nut-flour mixture. The brown-rice flour gives them a sandy texture, and the orange zest pairs perfectly with the pistachio flour.

Preheat oven to 350°F/180°C/Gas Mark 4. Spread the pistachios on a baking sheet and toast for 5 minutes, until light golden in color. Cool completely.

In the bowl of a food processor fitted with a metal blade, pulse pistachios, flour, sugar, salt, vanilla, and orange zest until very finely ground, about 1 minute. Transfer to a large bowl. Drop butter onto flour mixture. With a pastry cutter, cut in butter until mixture resembles coarse meal and begins to form a rough dough. (If the dough seems dry and is not holding together, add water, 1 tablespoon at a time, stirring with a fork, until the dough comes together.) Gather together with your hands, and lightly knead into a cohesive mass. Cover and chill overnight, for flours to hydrate.

Preheat oven to 350°F/180°C/Gas Mark 4. Line cookie sheets with parchment paper.

Using a small cookie scoop, such as #100, form 1¾ teaspoons of dough into ¾-inch balls. Place on prepared sheets, spacing about 1 inch apart. Bake for 10 to 14 minutes, until golden brown around the edges. Transfer cookies, still on parchment, to wire racks to cool completely.

Store cookies in an airtight container, at room temperature, for up to 5 days.

INGREDIENTS

1½ cups shelled, unsalted pistachios (186 grams)
1 cup plus 3 tablespoons gluten-free brown-rice flour (186 grams)
⅔ cup granulated sugar (133 grams)
¼ teaspoon fine sea salt
1 teaspoon pure vanilla extract
1 teaspoon finely chopped orange zest
9 tablespoons (1⅛ sticks) unsalted butter, room temperature, cut into ¼-inch cubes (133 grams)
1 to 3 tablespoons cold water, as needed

Spelt

Almond

Sesame Cookies

Chilling time: 30 minutes
Makes about 24 cookies

Simple, yet sophisticated, the texture of these elegant, buttery cookies is similar to shortbread, but the almond flour and sesame seeds give the cookies a subtle, nutty flavor. Use only high-quality, fresh sesame seeds.

In a medium bowl, whisk together flours, cream of tartar, salt, and sugar. Drop butter onto flour mixture. Using a pastry cutter, cut in butter until it resembles coarse meal. With a fork, stir in sesame seeds. Knead with hands until dough comes together. Cover and refrigerate for at least 30 minutes, so that dough is easier to work with.

Preheat oven to 350°F/180°C/ Gas Mark 4. Line cookie sheets with parchment paper.

Place extra sesame seeds in a small bowl. Using a medium scoop, such as #60, form 2 teaspoons of dough into 1-inch balls. Roll balls in extra sesame seeds. Place 1½ inches apart on prepared sheets and flatten to ⅓-inch thickness. Bake for 12 to 14 minutes, until pale brown. Cool for 2 minutes on cookie sheets. Transfer cookies, still on parchment, to wire racks to cool completely.

Store cookies in an airtight container, at room temperature, for up to 5 days.

INGREDIENTS

1 cup spelt flour (120 grams)
¾ cup almond flour (84 grams)
½ teaspoon cream of tartar
⅜ teaspoon fine sea salt
⅓ cup granulated sugar (67 grams)
8 tablespoons (1 stick) unsalted butter, cold, cut into ¼-inch cubes (113 grams)
2 tablespoons white sesame seeds, plus extra for rolling

Baker's Note: To enhance the nutty flavor, toast sesame seeds in a dry skillet on the stovetop, over moderate heat, for 2 to 3 minutes. Stir or shake frequently, until seeds are fragrant and a shade darker. Cool before using.

G-F

Oat

Peanut Butter Sandwiches

Chilling time: overnight
Makes about 50 unfilled cookies or 25 filled sandwich cookies

I love eating peanut butter cookies, and I love making peanut butter cookies. This cookie is made with the delightful combination of peanut butter and oat flour. The result is a gluten-free, melt-in-your-mouth cookie that is rich, with a smooth texture. I love them plain or as sandwiches, filled with yummy chocolate ganache or a tart jam.

In a medium bowl, sift together flour, salt, and baking powder. Set aside.

In the large bowl of an electric mixer, with speed set to high, beat butter and sugar for 1 to 2 minutes, until light and fluffy. Add egg. Beat for 1 to 2 minutes, until fluffy. Add peanut butter and vanilla. Beat to combine. Set mixer speed to low. Gradually add flour mixture. Mix until just combined. Cover and chill overnight, for flour to hydrate.

Preheat oven to 350°F/180°C/Gas Mark 4. Line cookie sheets with parchment paper.

Using a small cookie scoop, such as #100, form 1¾ teaspoons of dough into ¾-inch balls. Place them on prepared sheets, spacing about 1 inch apart. Flatten to ⅓- to ¼-inch thickness. Bake for 10 to 14 minutes, until golden brown and edges are a shade darker. Cool for 2 minutes on cookie sheets. Transfer cookies, still on parchment, to wire racks to cool completely.

To make the filling, place chopped chocolate in a small bowl. In a small saucepan, over low heat, heat cream until it simmers slightly. Remove from heat and pour over chocolate. Stir until smooth. Allow mixture to cool to room temperature, about 20 to 30 minutes, stirring occasionally, until it begins to thicken but not harden.

Just before serving, spread ½ teaspoon of filling over flat side of half of the cookies. Sandwich with another cookie. Serve filled cookies immediately.

Store unfilled cookies in an airtight container, at room temperature, for up to 5 days.

INGREDIENTS

1⅓ cups gluten-free oat flour (155 grams)
1 teaspoon fine sea salt
½ teaspoon baking powder
6 tablespoons (¾ stick) unsalted butter, room temperature (85 grams)
½ cup granulated sugar (100 grams)
1 large egg, room temperature
¾ cup unsalted, creamy peanut butter (192 grams)
1 teaspoon pure vanilla extract

Filling
2 ounces semisweet or bittersweet (60% cacao) chocolate, finely chopped (57 grams)
3 tablespoons heavy cream

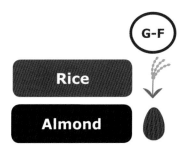

Orange-Scented Sugar Cookies

Chilling time: 2 hours
Makes about 30 cookies

These yummy, gluten-free, melt-in-your-mouth sugar cookies are light and flaky with a faint orange flavor. To reduce the grittiness of the brown-rice flour, use very finely milled gluten-free brown-rice flour available from companies such as King Arthur Flour.

Preheat oven to 350°F/180°C/Gas Mark 4. Line cookie sheets with parchment paper.

In a large bowl, sift together brown-rice flour, cream of tartar, baking soda, and salt. Whisk in almond flour and sugar. Drop butter onto mixture. Using a pastry cutter, cut in butter until it resembles coarse meal. Using a fork, stir in orange zest and extract. Using hands, knead dough and gather together. Cover and chill for 2 hours.

Using a small cookie scoop, such as #100, form 1¾ teaspoons of dough into ¾-inch balls. Roll tops in granulated sugar. Place on prepared sheets, spacing about 2 inches apart. Bake for 10 to 12 minutes, until pale golden brown. Tops will be cracked, and edges will be a shade darker. Cool for 2 minutes on cookie sheets. Transfer cookies, still on parchment, to wire racks to cool completely.

Store cookies in an airtight container, at room temperature, for up to one week.

INGREDIENTS

1 cup gluten-free brown-rice flour (160 grams)
½ teaspoon cream of tartar
¼ teaspoon baking soda
¼ teaspoon fine sea salt
¼ cup almond flour (28 grams)
½ cup granulated sugar (100 grams)
8 tablespoons (1 stick) unsalted butter, cold, cut into ¼-inch cubes (113 grams)
½ teaspoon packed, finely chopped or grated orange zest
½ teaspoon pure orange extract
Extra granulated sugar, for rolling

Baker's Note: This dough and these cookies do not freeze well. The rice flour absorbs too much moisture, and the cookies become doughy.

Cranberry-Walnut Cookies

Chilling time: 2 hours or overnight
Makes about 60 small cookies or 48 medium cookies

Loaded with cranberries and walnuts, these light and chewy cookies are the perfect oatmeal cookie. Set some aside for yourself, because they will vanish as soon as you put out a plate! For a fun alternative, replace the walnuts with toasted, shelled pumpkin seeds.

In a medium bowl, sift together flour, baking soda, baking powder, salt, and spices. Set aside.

In the large bowl of an electric mixer, with speed set to high, beat butter and sugars about 2 minutes, until light and fluffy. Add egg. Beat about 2 minutes, until light and fluffy. Add milk and vanilla. Mix until combined. Set mixer speed to low. Gradually add flour mixture. Mix until just combined. Add oats, walnuts, and cranberries. Mix until just combined. Cover and chill for 2 hours or as long as overnight, for flours to hydrate.

Preheat oven to 350°F/180°C/Gas Mark 4. Line cookie sheets with parchment paper.

For small cookies, using a small cookie scoop, such as #100, form 1¾ teaspoons of dough into ¾-inch balls. For medium cookies, using a medium cookie scoop, such as #60, form 2 teaspoons of dough into 1-inch balls. Place on prepared sheets, spacing about 2 inches apart. Bake for 10 to 12 minutes, until golden brown. Cool for 2 minutes on cookie sheets. Transfer cookies, still on parchment, to wire racks to cool completely.

Store cookies in an airtight container, at room temperature, for up to 5 days.

INGREDIENTS

¾ cup plus 1 tablespoon spelt flour (98 grams)
½ teaspoon baking soda
½ teaspoon baking powder
¼ teaspoon salt
¼ teaspoon ground ginger
¼ teaspoon ground cinnamon
8 tablespoons (1 stick) unsalted butter, room temperature (113 grams)
¼ cup plus 2 tablespoons packed dark brown sugar (83 grams)
¼ cup plus 2 tablespoons granulated sugar (75 grams)
1 large egg, room temperature
1 tablespoon whole milk
1 teaspoon pure vanilla extract
1½ cups old-fashioned rolled oats (136 grams)
¾ scant cup toasted walnuts, chopped (82 grams)
½ cup dried cranberries, coarsely chopped (80 grams)

Baker's Note: Use old-fashioned rolled oats rather than quick-cooking oats to give cookies a more rustic look. Do not use instant oatmeal in cookies, as it does not provide the proper texture.

Blueberry Jammers

Makes 16 bars

These homey, jam-filled wonders are great for take-along lunches or camping trips. One taste tester suggested renaming these cookies "Blueberry Jammies," because eating them is like slipping into your favorite pajamas after a long day. I use Stonewall Kitchen's Wild Maine Blueberry Jam, but any high-quality wild blueberry jam will do.

Preheat oven to 350°F/180°C/Gas Mark 4. Line an 8x8-inch baking pan with aluminum foil, leaving a 2-inch overhang on two opposite edges. Cut a piece of parchment paper to fit the bottom of the pan. Place parchment on top of foil. Lightly oil the parchment and the sides of the pan.

In the bowl of a food processor, combine flour, oats, sugar, and salt. Pulse for 20 to 30 seconds. Add butter and water. Pulse just until the dough begins to gather together and holds together when pressed. Divide the dough mixture in half. Press one-half of the dough evenly in the bottom of the prepared baking pan. Put remaining dough aside.

Spread jam evenly over dough. With your fingers, sprinkle the remaining dough evenly on top of jam, covering completely. Using a rubber spatula, press down firmly but gently. Bake for 35 to 40 minutes, until golden brown. Place on wire rack and cool completely in the pan. When ready to serve, using the foil overhang, lift uncut bars from pan. Cut into 16 servings.

Store bars in an airtight container, at room temperature, for up to 3 days.

INGREDIENTS

1 cup white whole-wheat flour (130 grams)
1 cup old-fashioned rolled oats (90 grams)
¼ cup packed light brown sugar (55 grams)
¼ teaspoon salt
8 tablespoons (1 stick) unsalted butter, cold, cut into ¼-inch cubes (113 grams)
1 tablespoon cold water
1 cup wild blueberry jam, room temperature, stirred (320 grams)

G-F

Pistachio-Almond Meringues

Pistachio

Almond

Makes about 42 cookies

Inspired to make a gluten-free pistachio cookie for my friend Laura, these light and nutty cookies hit the mark. As with most nut meringues, they are airy, crumbly, and slightly chewy. The addition of almond flour tempers the pistachio flavor.

Preheat oven to 275°F/140°C/ Gas Mark 1. Line cookie sheets with parchment paper.

In a medium bowl, whisk together ground pistachios and almond flour. Set aside.

In the small bowl of an electric mixer, with speed set to high, beat egg whites and salt about 2 minutes, until soft peaks form. Gradually add sugar. Beat 2 to 3 minutes, until stiff peaks form. Using a rubber spatula, carefully fold in nut mixture in 3 or 4 batches, being careful not to deflate the batter.

Drop 2 teaspoons of mixture onto prepared sheets, spacing 2 inches apart. Smooth out any peaks. Bake for 25 to 30 minutes, until pale golden brown and firm to touch. Place cookie sheets on wire racks and cool completely.

Store cookies in an airtight container, at room temperature, for up to 1 week.

INGREDIENTS

¾ cup shelled, unsalted pistachios, ground (95 grams)
¾ cup almond flour (84 grams)
2 large egg whites, room temperature
⅛ teaspoon salt
½ cup superfine sugar (100 grams)

Baker's Note: Rinse mixing bowl with warm water and dry thoroughly before beating the eggs. The warmth from the bowl will help the eggs form peaks faster. If you wish, you can use a #60 scoop to place the batter on the cookie sheets. If you want a stronger pistachio flavor, change the proportion to 1 cup pistachios (125 grams) and ½ cup almond flour (56 grams).

G-F

Coconut

Coconut-Crazy Macaroon Sandwiches

Makes about 48 unfilled cookies or 24 filled sandwich cookies

Love coconut? You will double love these coconut macaroon treats, sandwiched with a creamy coconut filling. The chewy, rich, deliciously coconut-y cookies are simple to make and delicious on their own. When sandwiched, the contrast in textures between the cookie and the filling makes them absolutely decadent.

Preheat oven to 350°F/180°C/ Gas Mark 4. Line cookie sheets with parchment paper.

In a medium bowl, whisk together coconuts, sugar, and salt. Using a large spoon, mix in vanilla. Add beaten egg whites and water. Mix well, until mixture is moistened and starts to hold together.

Using a small cookie scoop, such as #100, form 1¾ teaspoons of dough into ¾-inch balls. Place on prepared sheets, spacing 1½ inches apart. Bake for 12 to 15 minutes, until bottoms are golden and tops turn golden brown. Cool for 1 minute on cookie sheets. Transfer the cookies, still on parchment, to wire racks to cool completely.

To prepare the filling, in the small bowl of an electric mixer, with speed set to medium, beat cream cheese and cream about 1 minute, until smooth and creamy. Reduce mixer speed to low. Add powdered sugar. Mix about 2 minutes, until combined. Add coconut. Mix until just combined.

Spread ½ teaspoon of mixture over flat side of half of the cookies. Sandwich with another cookie. Serve filled cookies immediately. Store any extra filling in the refrigerator.

Store unfilled cookies in an airtight container, at room temperature, for up to 5 days.

INGREDIENTS

2 cups shredded sweetened coconut, finely chopped (240 grams)
1 cup unsweetened coconut, finely chopped (80 grams)
⅔ cup granulated sugar (133 grams)
¼ teaspoon salt
1½ teaspoons pure vanilla extract
2 large egg whites, lightly beaten
2 teaspoons water

Filling

2 tablespoons cream cheese, room temperature (28 grams)
3 tablespoons heavy cream, room temperature (54 grams)
¾ cup powdered sugar (94 grams)
¼ cup plus 2 tablespoons shredded sweetened coconut (46 grams)

Baker's Note: For a less sweet filling, replace 3 tablespoons of sweetened coconut (23 grams) with 3 tablespoons of unsweetened coconut (15 grams).

For the Love of Maple and Pecans

Chilling time: overnight
Makes about 50 cookies

These nutty, buttery, crispy, melt-in-your-mouth cookies are "pecan pie embodied in a cookie." The deep pecan flavor is enhanced by the pure maple extract and dark brown sugar. The texture is light and airy. To heighten the flavor, and impart the right amount of sweetness, sprinkle with raw sugar before baking.

In a medium bowl, sift together flours, baking powder, and salt. Set aside.

In the large bowl of an electric mixer, with speed set to high, beat butter and sugars for 1 to 2 minutes, until light and fluffy. Add extracts. Mix until thoroughly combined. Reduce mixer speed to low. Add flour mixture in batches, alternating with ground pecans. Mix until just combined and crumbly. Gather together with hands. Divide dough into 2 portions and shape each into a disk. Wrap each disk in wax paper or plastic wrap and chill overnight, for flours to hydrate.

Preheat oven to 350°F/180°C/Gas Mark 4. Line cookie sheets with parchment paper.

Roll dough, one disk at a time, between sheets of wax paper to ¼-inch thickness. Cut with 1-inch round cookie cutter. Place on prepared sheets, spacing 1 inch apart. Sprinkle with raw sugar. If dough becomes too gooey to handle, return to refrigerator for a few minutes to firm. Bake for 10 to 12 minutes, until light golden brown. Cool for 1 minute on cookie sheets. Transfer cookies, still on parchment, to wire racks to cool completely.

Store cookies in an airtight container, at room temperature, for up to one week.

INGREDIENTS

¾ cup spelt flour (90 grams)
½ cup oat flour (60 grams)
½ teaspoon baking powder
¼ teaspoon salt
8 tablespoons (1 stick) unsalted butter, room temperature (113 grams)
2½ tablespoons granulated sugar (31 grams)
2½ tablespoons packed dark brown sugar (34 grams)
½ teaspoon pure vanilla extract
⅛ teaspoon pure maple extract
½ cup toasted whole pecans, finely ground (55 grams)
Raw sugar, such as turbindo, for sprinkling

Baker's Note: Toast pecans for 5 minutes at 350°F/180°C/Gas Mark 4 to bring out their full flavor.

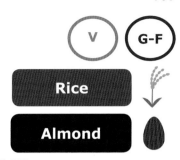

Cinnamon Cookies

Makes about 36 cookies

Whenever I create a vegan cookie, I call on my friend Anna to evaluate the flavor and crumb. After a few iterations, she declared these delicious! You will find that these gluten-free, vegan cookies are delightfully crispy with a lovely texture.

Preheat oven to 350°F/180°C/Gas Mark 4. Line cookie sheets with parchment paper.

In a large bowl, sift together brown-rice flour, cream of tartar, baking soda, salt, and cinnamon. Whisk in almond flour and sugar. Using a large spoon, mix in olive oil, until combined. Mixture will resemble damp sand.

Add coconut milk. Stir to combine. Let sit at room temperature for at least 15 minutes, for flours to hydrate.

Using a small cookie scoop, such as #100, form 1¾ teaspoons of dough into ¾-inch balls. Place on prepared sheets, spacing about 2 inches apart. Flatten to ⅓-inch thickness. Bake for 10 to 12 minutes, until golden brown and firm to touch. Cool for 2 minutes on cookie sheets. Transfer cookies, still on parchment, to wire racks to cool completely.

Store cookies in an airtight container, at room temperature, for up to one week.

INGREDIENTS

1 cup gluten-free brown-rice flour (160 grams)

1 teaspoon cream of tartar

½ teaspoon baking soda

¼ teaspoon fine sea salt

¾ teaspoon ground cinnamon

¼ cup almond flour (28 grams)

½ cup granulated sugar (100 grams)

¼ cup plus 1 tablespoon high-quality extra-light or extra-virgin olive oil

⅓ cup unsweetened coconut milk, stirred

Baker's Note: Olive oil cookies bake differently than butter-based cookies. They will appear very moist at first and become firm to touch while baking. This dough and these cookies do not freeze well. The rice flour absorbs too much moisture, and the cookies become doughy.

GULF of MEXICO

PACIFIC OCEAN

Corn   Amaranth

Mesoamerica

Mesoamerica is one of six areas in the world where ancient civilizations arose independently. This civilization, along with the comparable Andean civilization in Peru, constitutes a New World counterpart to the ancient civilizations of Egypt, Mesopotamia, the Indus Valley, and China. It is believed to be the first region in the world where writing developed.

Mesoamerica was home to several pre-Columbian societies, beginning with the Olmec around 1600 BC. It extended from what today is central Mexico to Belize, Guatemala, El Salvador, Honduras, Nicaragua, and northern Costa Rica.

Evidence of the domestication of maize, today called corn, has been found in central Mexico and in Guatemala. These sites, dating back to 5100 BC, show evidence of teosinte, the ancestor of maize. The domestication of maize, along with beans, squash, and chilies, caused a transition from hunter-gatherer tribal groups to sedentary agricultural villages in this region. This area of the world, with a rich history and culture, changed dramatically when the Spanish conquered the region in the sixteenth century.

The recipes in this chapter focus on two gluten-free grains that originated in Mesoamerica: corn and amaranth.

Top row: cornmeal; bottom row: amaranth flour, corn flour

Cornmeal

Corn, as we know it today, is a human invention, created over centuries of domestication and hybridization. Teosinte, the earliest known ancestor to maize or corn, is a wild grass. It is believed that maize evolved from a crossbreeding of teosinte and other grasses.

A staple of North and South American food production, corn has many more varieties than other cereal crops due to its ability to cross-pollinate easily. Corn production plays a major role in the economy of the United States, where 95 percent of corn farmlands are family-owned. Today corn is grown predominately in central Iowa and Illinois and has many forms and many uses.

Cornmeal is ground dried corn. It comes in a range of grinds from very coarse to fine and is sometimes called uncooked polenta. Fine-grain cornmeal is used most often in baked goods. However, because of its gritty texture and lack of gluten, it is usually mixed with other flours to give it structure and lift. The underlying sweetness of corn provides a good pairing with fruits, such as cherries, blueberries, or apricots.

Corn Flour

Corn flour is very finely ground whole-grain cornmeal. It is not cornstarch, which is the white, powdered endosperm (heart) of the corn kernel.

There are several varieties of corn flour, such as masa harina, that are treated with lime alkali. These are not suitable for the cookie recipes in this book. Instead, use very finely ground untreated corn flour.

Amaranth Flour

Amaranth, known to the Aztecs as huauhtli, is a seed. It was cultivated in Central America as long as seven thousand years ago. Before the Spanish conquest, it was a staple of the Aztec diet and may have represented up to 80 percent of their caloric consumption. Amaranth's cultivation ended when the conquistador Hernando Cortez decreed that anyone growing the crop would be put to death.

Amaranth is considered a pseudo-grain because of its nutritional profile. It has the highest level of protein of all grains and is high in lysine, which many grains lack. Interest in the grain was revived in the 1970s, when an article in *Science* described amaranth as "the crop of the future." Today, several species of amaranth are raised in Asia and the Americas.

Amaranth flour is made from finely ground amaranth seeds. It is gluten-free, with a mild, nutty flavor and grassy notes. In baking, it is usually used in combination with wheat flour. Amaranth flour can be found online at Nuts.com or from Bob's Red Mill.

Cornmeal

Spelt

Citrus Cornmeal Cookies

Chilling time: 1 hour
Makes about 60 small cookies or about 42 medium cookies

Everyone loves these crunchy citrus cookies. To quote one of my taste testers, "The orange and lemon add another dimension to the sweetness of the cookie. Cornmeal rocks."

In a medium bowl, sift together cornmeal, spelt, and salt. Whisk in the sugar. Drop butter onto flour mixture. Using a pastry cutter, cut in butter until mixture resembles coarse meal. Using a fork, mix in lemon and orange zests. Stir in egg yolk, combining thoroughly. Stir in almonds. With hands, knead dough gently and form into a disk. Wrap in wax paper or plastic wrap and chill for at least 1 hour, to make dough easier to roll.

Preheat oven to 350°F/180°C/ Gas Mark 4. Line cookie sheets with parchment paper.

Roll dough between sheets of wax paper to ⅓- to ¼-inch thickness. Cut with 1-inch or 1½-inch round cookie cutter. Place on prepared sheets, spacing about 1 inch apart. Bake for 8 to 10 minutes for 1-inch cookies or for 10 to 12 minutes for 1½-inch cookies, until light golden brown. Cool for 1 minute on cookie sheets. Transfer cookies, still on parchment, to wire racks to cool completely.

Store cookies in an airtight container, at room temperature, for up to one week.

INGREDIENTS

⅔ cup finely ground yellow cornmeal (100 grams)
⅔ cup spelt flour (80 grams)
⅛ teaspoon fine sea salt
½ cup granulated sugar (100 grams)
8 tablespoons (1 stick) unsalted butter, cold, cut into ¼-inch cubes (113 grams)
1 teaspoon packed finely chopped or grated lemon zest
1 teaspoon packed finely chopped or grated orange zest
1 large egg yolk, room temperature
½ cup slivered, blanched almonds, finely chopped (56 grams)

Baker's Note: If dough is too stiff to roll, let it sit for a few minutes at room temperature. To enhance the citrus flavor, add ¼ teaspoon of pure lemon or pure orange extract along with the citrus zests.

Walnut-Amaranth Minis

Chilling time: overnight
Makes about 42 cookies

Amaranth is actually a seed. It has an interesting grassy smell and was used by the ancient Aztecs in religious ceremonies. These buttery cookies are made with this ancient grain and can be coated with amaranth seeds for a lovely, crunchy texture. Pecans can be substituted for walnuts, if desired.

In the bowl of a food processor fitted with a metal blade, pulse walnuts and 2 tablespoons of sugar for about 15 seconds, until the mixture looks sandy and nuts are finely ground. Set aside.

In a medium bowl, sift together flours and salt. Set aside.

In the large bowl of an electric mixer, with speed set to high, beat butter 1 to 2 minutes, until smooth. Add remaining sugar. Beat 1 to 2 minutes, until fluffy and smooth. Add egg yolk and vanilla. Beat about 1 minute, until well blended. Reduce mixer speed to low. Mix in nut mixture. Gradually add flour mixture. Mix until just incorporated. Cover and chill overnight, for flours to hydrate.

Preheat oven to 350°F/180°C/ Gas Mark 4. Line cookie sheets with parchment paper.

If coating with seeds, place the amaranth seeds in a small bowl. Using a small cookie scoop, such as #100, form 1¾ teaspoons of dough into ¾-inch balls. Roll each ball in amaranth seeds, if desired, gently pressing to adhere if needed. Place on prepared sheets, spacing about 2 inches apart. Flatten to ⅓-inch thickness. Bake for 10 to 12 minutes, until edges are golden brown. Transfer cookies, still on parchment paper, to wire racks to cool completely. Cookies will crisp as they cool.

Store cookies in an airtight container, at room temperature, for up to 5 days.

INGREDIENTS

1 scant cup toasted walnuts (114 grams)
½ cup granulated sugar (100 grams), divided
¾ cup white whole-wheat flour (102 grams)
¼ cup amaranth flour (34 grams)
¼ teaspoon fine sea salt
8 tablespoons (1 stick) unsalted butter, room temperature (113 grams)
1 large egg yolk, room temperature
1 teaspoon pure vanilla extract
¼ cup amaranth seeds, for rolling, optional (52 grams)

Baker's Note: Toast walnuts at 350°F/180°C/ Gas Mark 4 for 5 to 7 minutes, to bring out their nutty flavor.

Corn Crisps

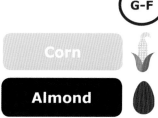

Chilling time: overnight
Makes about 30 cookies

These easy, one-bowl cookies are crispy, crunchy, and light with a delicately sweet corn flavor. The finely ground corn flour makes them just a little bit chewy. One of my taste testers was astounded when I told him that they are gluten-free.

In a medium bowl, whisk together flours, cornstarch, baking soda, and salt. Whisk in sugar. Drop butter onto flour mixture. With a pastry cutter, cut in butter until dough resembles coarse meal. Using a fork, mix in vanilla, combining thoroughly. Gather together, cover, and chill dough overnight.

Preheat oven to 350°F/180°C/ Gas Mark 4. Line cookie sheets with parchment paper.

Using a small cookie scoop, such as #100, form 1¾ teaspoons of dough into ¾-inch balls. Place on prepared sheets, spacing about 2½ inches apart. Don't crowd the cookies as they will spread considerably while baking. Bake for 10 to 12 minutes, until edges are golden brown. Cool for 2 minutes on cookie sheets. Transfer cookies, still on parchment, to wire racks to cool completely.

Store cookies in an airtight container, at room temperature, for up to 5 days.

INGREDIENTS

⅔ cup whole-grain corn flour (**77 grams**)
⅓ cup almond flour (**38 grams**)
2 tablespoons cornstarch (**16 grams**)
¼ teaspoon baking soda
¼ teaspoon fine sea salt
½ cup granulated sugar (**100 grams**)
8 tablespoons (1 stick) unsalted butter, cold, cut into ¼-inch cubes (**226 grams**)
1 teaspoon pure vanilla extract

Corn

Spelt

Walnut-Orange Bars

Makes 16 bars

Walnut and orange make these fragrant and subtly perfumed cookies one of my favorites. They are made with whole-grain corn flour and maple syrup, giving them a lovely color and a complex flavor. They are perfect as a breakfast bar or on your dessert plate.

Preheat oven to 350°F/180°C/Gas Mark 4. Line an 8x8-inch baking pan with aluminum foil, leaving a 2-inch overhang on two opposite edges. Cut a piece of parchment paper to fit bottom of pan. Lightly butter parchment and sides of pan.

In a medium bowl, sift together flours, baking soda, and salt. Set aside.

In a small saucepan, over low heat, melt butter. Cool for 5 minutes.

In the large bowl of an electric mixer, with speed set to high, beat melted butter, sugar, and maple syrup about 2 minutes, until creamy. Add eggs and vanilla. Beat about 2 minutes, until fluffy. Mix in orange zest until distributed throughout dough. Reduce mixer speed to low. Mix in flour mixture until combined. Add walnuts. Mix until just combined.

Pour batter evenly into prepared pan. Smooth top. Bake for 20 to 25 minutes, until top is golden brown and firm to touch. It will pull away slightly from the sides. Place on wire rack and cool completely in the pan. When ready to serve, using the foil overhang, lift uncut bars from pan. Cut into 16 servings.

Store bars in an airtight container, at room temperature, for up to 5 days.

INGREDIENTS

½ cup plus 1 tablespoon whole-grain corn flour (65 grams)
½ cup spelt flour (60 grams)
½ teaspoon baking soda
⅛ teaspoon salt
8 tablespoons (1 stick) unsalted butter (113 grams)
¾ cup packed light brown sugar (165 grams)
2 tablespoons maple syrup, Grade A medium amber or dark amber (40 grams)
2 large eggs, room temperature
1 teaspoon pure vanilla extract
1 tablespoon finely chopped or grated orange zest
¾ cup coarsely chopped walnuts (89 grams)

Chocolate-Chip and Cherry Cookies

Chilling time: overnight
Makes about 30 cookies

My biggest chocolate-chip cookie fan just happens to be my husband. He loves these sweet, tart, dark chocolate-chip cookies. I think it must be the bittersweet (60% cacao) chocolate chips that I use that makes them so appealing.

In a medium bowl, sift together flours, baking powder, baking soda, and salt. Set aside.

In the large bowl of an electric mixer, with speed set to high, beat butter, sugar, and vanilla about 2 minutes, until fluffy. Add egg. Beat about 1 minute, until light and fluffy. Reduce mixer speed to low. Gradually add the flour mixture. Mix until just combined. Add chocolate chips and cherries. Mix until just combined. Cover and chill overnight, for flours to hydrate.

Preheat oven to 350°F/180°C/ Gas Mark 4. Line cookie sheets with parchment paper.

Using a medium cookie scoop, such as #40, form 4 teaspoons of dough into 1⅜-inch balls. Place on prepared sheets, spacing about 2½ inches apart. Bake for 12 to 14 minutes, until golden brown. Cool for 2 minutes on cookie sheets. Transfer cookies, still on parchment, to wire racks to cool completely.

Store cookies in an airtight container, at room temperature, for up to five days.

INGREDIENTS

⅔ cup white whole-wheat flour (87 grams)
⅓ cup amaranth flour (40 grams)
¾ teaspoon baking powder
⅛ teaspoon baking soda
⅛ teaspoon fine sea salt
10 tablespoons (1¼ sticks) unsalted butter, room temperature (141 grams)
¾ cup packed dark brown sugar (165 grams)
1 teaspoon pure vanilla extract
1 large egg, room temperature
1¼ cups bittersweet (60% cacao) chocolate chips (204 grams)
¾ cup dried sour cherries, coarsely chopped (120 grams)

Baker's Note: After removing dough from refrigerator, let it sit for a few minutes to soften before scooping.

Pastry

Cornmeal

Jam Thumbprints

Chilling time: overnight
Makes about 28 cookies

This traditional jam thumbprint cookie, made with whole-wheat pastry flour and cornmeal, is tender and buttery. It is good with either sweet or tart jam. As with many whole-grain cookies, the texture of this cookie softens twenty-four hours after baking as the outer layer of bran breaks down.

In a medium bowl, sift together flour, cornmeal, baking powder, and salt. Set aside.

In the large bowl of an electric mixer, with speed set to high, beat butter and powdered sugar for 1 to 2 minutes, until light and fluffy. Add egg yolk and vanilla. Beat until just combined. Set mixer speed to low. Mix in flour mixture until just incorporated. Cover and chill overnight, for flours to hydrate.

Preheat oven to 350°F/180°C/ Gas Mark 4. Line cookie sheets with parchment paper.

Using a small cookie scoop, such as #100, form 1¾ teaspoons of dough into ¾-inch balls. Place on prepared sheets, spacing about 1 inch apart. Press a thumbprint, about ¼-inch deep, into the center of each cookie. Spoon ¼ teaspoon of fruit preserve into the thumbprint. Bake for 10 to 12 minutes, until edges are golden brown. Cool for 2 minutes on cookie sheets. Transfer cookies, still on parchment, to wire racks to cool completely.

Layer cookies between wax paper or parchment paper and store in an airtight container, at room temperature, for up to 5 days.

INGREDIENTS

¾ cup plus 2 tablespoons whole-wheat pastry flour (114 grams)
¼ cup finely ground yellow cornmeal (38 grams)
¼ teaspoon baking powder
¼ teaspoon fine sea salt
8 tablespoons (1 stick) unsalted butter, room temperature (113 grams)
¼ cup powdered sugar (31 grams)
1 large egg yolk, room temperature
½ teaspoon pure vanilla extract
¼ cup apricot, raspberry, or cherry preserves (76 grams)

Pastry

Cornmeal

Almond

Blueberry-Cornmeal Cookies

Chilling time: 2 hours or overnight
Makes about 30 cookies

My friend Brooks tells me that these cookies are one of his favorite "breakfast cookies." It must be the sweet, dried wild blueberries and the light texture that earn them this accolade. The tender crumb is the result of the crunchy cornmeal and rich, flaky almond meal. These soft, sweet cookies are a delicious change of pace when you want to explore something new, for breakfast or any time of day. For a less sweet cookie, you can skip the glaze.

In a medium bowl, sift together pastry flour, baking soda, and salt. Whisk in cornmeal and almond flour. Set aside.

In the large bowl of an electric mixer, with speed set to high, beat butter, sugars, and vanilla about 2 minutes, until light and fluffy. Add egg. Beat 1 to 2 minutes, until fluffy. Set mixer speed to low. Gradually add flour mixture, mixing until just combined. Add blueberries. Mix until just combined. Cover and chill for 2 hours or overnight.

Preheat the oven to 350°F/180°C/ Gas Mark 4. Line cookie sheets with parchment paper.

Using a medium cookie scoop, such as #60, form 2 teaspoons of dough into 1-inch balls. Place on prepared sheets, spacing about 2 inches apart. Flatten to ⅓-inch thickness. Bake for 8 to 12 minutes, until golden brown. Cool for 2 minutes on cookie sheets. Transfer cookies, still on parchment, to wire racks to cool completely.

When cookies have cooled, prepare the glaze. In a small bowl, combine all glaze ingredients. Using a large spoon, mix until smooth. Using a pastry brush, brush the top of each cookie with glaze. Allow glaze to dry before serving or storing.

Store cookies in an airtight container, at room temperature, for up to 3 days.

INGREDIENTS

⅔ cup whole-wheat pastry flour (87 grams)
½ teaspoon baking soda
¼ teaspoon fine sea salt
¼ cup finely ground yellow cornmeal (38 grams)
⅓ cup almond flour (38 grams)
8 tablespoons (1 stick) unsalted butter, room temperature (113 grams)
¼ cup granulated sugar (50 grams)
1½ tablespoons packed light brown sugar (21 grams)
1 teaspoon pure vanilla extract
1 large egg, room temperature
½ cup dried wild blueberries (92 grams)

Glaze
½ cup powdered sugar (63 grams)
½ teaspoon pure vanilla extract
1½ tablespoons boiling water

Spelt

Corn

Dirty-Blond Blondies

Makes 16 bars

The inspiration for these delicately sweet, unbelievable blondies came from my friends Richard and Beth, who love all of my cookies, in all of their forms. These blondies are light and slightly gooey, with a crispy top and just enough sweetness. Be sure to use corn flour, which is very finely ground corn, and not cornmeal.

Preheat oven to 350°F/180°C/Gas Mark 4. Line an 8x8-inch baking pan with aluminum foil, leaving a 2-inch overhang on two opposite edges. Cut parchment to fit bottom of pan. Lightly oil the parchment and the sides of the pan.

In a medium bowl, sift together flours. Set aside.

In the large bowl of an electric mixer, with speed set to high, beat butter, sugar, coffee extract or espresso powder, and vanilla about 2 minutes, until light and fluffy. Add eggs. Beat about 2 minutes, until fluffy. Reduce mixer speed to low. Gradually add flour mixture. Mix until combined. Add white chocolate and pecans. Mix until just combined.

Pour batter evenly into prepared pan. Smooth top. Bake for 20 to 30 minutes, until top is golden brown and shiny. It will pull away slightly from the sides, and top will be firm to touch. Place on wire rack and cool completely in the pan. When ready to serve, using the foil overhang, lift uncut bars from pan. Cut into 16 servings.

Store bars in an airtight container, at room temperature or in the refrigerator, for up to 3 days.

INGREDIENTS

½ cup spelt flour (60 grams)
½ cup whole-grain corn flour (58 grams)
8 tablespoons (1 stick) unsalted butter, room temperature (113 grams)
1¼ cup packed light brown sugar (275 grams)
½ teaspoon pure coffee extract or instant espresso powder
1 teaspoon pure vanilla extract
2 large eggs, room temperature
1 scant cup white chocolate chips or 5½ ounces white chocolate, coarsely chopped (156 grams)
¾ cup coarsely chopped pecans (82 grams)

Baker's Note: Blondie will settle and collapse a little in the center while cooling.

Polenta-Apricot Cookies

Makes about 24 cookies

Soft, yet crunchy, and redolent of corn, these cookies are sure to be a ten if you like polenta. I use Mediterranean apricots because of their exceptional plumpness, but California apricots work as well.

Preheat oven to 350°F/180°C/Gas Mark 4. Line cookie sheets with parchment paper.

In a medium bowl, sift together spelt, cornmeal, baking powder, and salt. Whisk in sugars. Drop butter onto flour mixture. Using a pastry cutter, cut in butter until mixture resembles coarse meal.

In a small bowl, beat egg to twice its volume. Add vanilla. Pour egg mixture over dough. Using a fork, mix until thoroughly combined. Stir in apricots, until dispersed throughout dough.

Using a medium cookie scoop, such as #60, form 2 teaspoons of dough into 1-inch balls. Place on prepared sheets, spacing about 2 inches apart. Flatten to ⅓-inch thickness. If desired, sprinkle with a little raw sugar. Bake for 10 to 12 minutes, until golden brown and edges are a shade darker. Transfer cookies, still on parchment, to wire racks to cool completely.

Store cookies in an airtight container, at room temperature, for up to one week.

INGREDIENTS

¾ cup spelt flour (90 grams)
½ cup finely ground yellow cornmeal (75 grams)
½ teaspoon baking powder
⅛ teaspoon fine sea salt
¼ cup granulated sugar (50 grams)
1½ tablespoons packed light brown sugar (21 grams)
4 tablespoons (½ stick) unsalted butter, cold, cut into ¼-inch cubes (57 grams)
1 large egg, room temperature
¾ teaspoon pure vanilla extract
⅓ cup finely diced dried apricots (59 grams)
Raw sugar, such as turbindo, for sprinkling (optional)

Spelt

Amaranth

Honey and Cream Cookies

Chilling time: 2 hours or overnight
Makes about 50 cookies

These tender, crumbly cookies are made with the ancient grain amaranth. Amaranth has a cut-grass flavor that is tamed by the honey. My taste testers said the aroma reminded them of sweet clover.

In a medium bowl, sift together flours and salt. Drop butter onto flour mixture. Using a pastry cutter, cut in the butter until mixture resembles coarse meal. Using a fork, mix in honey and cream, combining thoroughly, until a stiff dough is formed. Shape dough into a disk and wrap in wax paper or plastic wrap.

Chill for at least 2 hours or overnight.

Preheat oven to 350°F/180°C/ Gas Mark 4. Line cookie sheets with parchment paper.

Roll dough between sheets of wax paper to ¼-inch thickness. Cut with 1-inch round cookie cutter. Place on prepared sheets, spacing about 1 inch apart. Bake for 8 to 10 minutes, until golden brown. Transfer cookies, still on parchment, to wire racks to cool completely.

Store cookies in an airtight container, at room temperature, for up to one week.

INGREDIENTS

1 cup spelt flour (120 grams)
⅓ cup amaranth flour (40 grams)
⅛ teaspoon fine sea salt
8 tablespoons (1 stick) unsalted butter, cold, cut into ¼-inch cubes (113 grams)
2 tablespoons organic honey (34 grams)
2 tablespoons heavy cream

Baker's Note: If dough is chilled overnight, let it sit about 5 minutes to soften before rolling.

Baking Resources

Bob's Red Mill Natural Foods
5000 SE International Way
Milwaukie, OR 97222
800-349-2173
www.bobsredmill.com
Specialty flours

Boyajian Incorporated
144 Will Drive
Canton, MA 02021
800-965-0665
www.boyajianinc.com
Extracts and oils

Cookietins.com
PO Box 1351
Bellaire, TX 77402
832-518-2800
www.e-cookietins.com
Food-safe storage containers

Hodgson Mill, Inc.
1100 Stevens Avenue
Effingham, IL 62401
800-525-0177
www.hodgsonmill.com
Specialty flours

King Arthur Flour Company
135 US Route 5 South
Norwich, VT 05055
800-827-6836
www.kingarthurflour.com
Specialty flours and baking supplies

Nuts.com
125 Moen Street
Cranford, NJ 07016
800-558-6887
www.nuts.com
Specialty flours, nuts, and dried fruits

Penzeys Spices
12001 W Capitol Drive
Wauwatosa, WI 53222
800-741-7787
www.penzeys.com
Extracts and spices

Wilton Industries
2240 W. 75th St.
Woodridge, Il. 60517
800-794-5866
www.wilton.com
Food-safe storage containers

Index

GULF of
MEXICO

PACIFIC
OCEAN

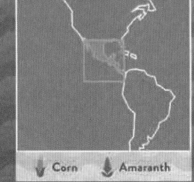

↓ Corn   ↓ Amaranth